D0411149

weekends with friends

weekends with friends

Maxine Clark

photography by Noel Murphy

RYLAND
PETERS
& SMALL

LONDON NEW YORK

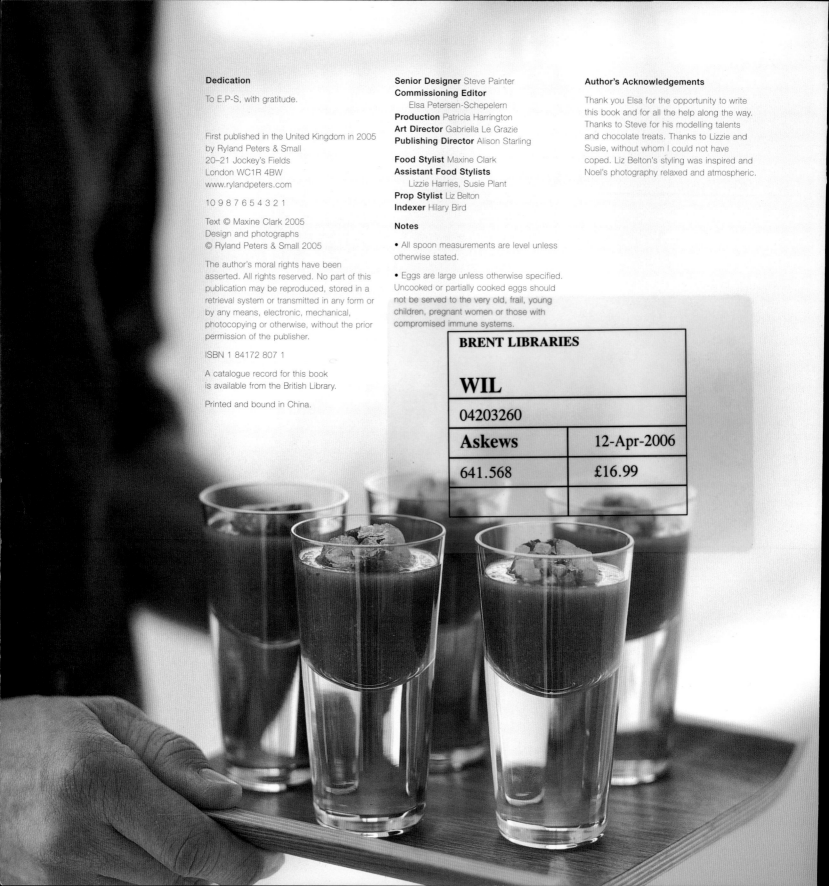

Dedication

To E.P-S, with gratitude.

First published in the United Kingdom in 2005
by Ryland Peters & Small
20–21 Jockey's Fields
London WC1R 4BW
www.rylandpeters.com

10 9 8 7 6 5 4 3 2 1

ISBN 1 84172 807 1

A catalogue record for this book
is available from the British Library.

Printed and bound in China.

Senior Designer Steve Painter
Commissioning Editor
    Elsa Petersen-Schepelern
Production Patricia Harrington
Art Director Gabriella Le Grazie
Publishing Director Alison Starling

Food Stylist Maxine Clark
Assistant Food Stylists
    Lizzie Harries, Susie Plant
Prop Stylist Liz Belton
Indexer Hilary Bird

Notes

• All spoon measurements are level unless
otherwise stated.

• Eggs are large unless otherwise specified.
Uncooked or partially cooked eggs should
not be served to the very old, frail, young
children, pregnant women or those with
compromised immune systems.

Author's Acknowledgements

Thank you Elsa for the opportunity to write
this book and for all the help along the way.
Thanks to Steve for his modelling talents
and chocolate treats. Thanks to Lizzie and
Susie, without whom I could not have
coped. Liz Belton's styling was inspired and
Noel's photography relaxed and atmospheric.

contents

planning the weekend

Don't you just envy friends who seem like natural-born hosts, cool, calm and collected and completely unfazed by numbers? Well, we can all be like that with a little organization and forward thinking. Half an hour's planning and list-making will save so much time and anxiety when guests arrive, and will do wonders for your confidence. So take some time out and sit down quietly with a notepad and pen and start at the beginning.

Planning Ahead

When will everyone arrive, and what will the first meal be? Will it just be a cup of tea and a cake or a drink and some nibbles? Start here and draw up a list of meals and snacks, adding in drinks as well. From this, expand the list into menus, following the Ten Golden Rules on pages 8–9. Remember, the reason for getting together in the first place is to enjoy each other's company in relaxed surroundings, enhanced by some simple and delicious food and drink, so don't put pressure on yourself to be a top chef – this isn't the time! Above all, you should make the cooking and eating fun and part of the total experience, and don't let it become a chore. Make use of the oven when it's on and cook more than one thing at a time, or cook double quantities to keep for later, or turn into another meal.

Shopping Ahead

Try to do all the shopping in one go, making a note of anything you will still have to buy later. Divide your shopping list into categories – Dry Goods; Fruit and Vegetables; Meat, Poultry and Fish; Dairy; and Miscellaneous. This will make the shopping easier. At the checkout, pack all the refrigerator items together with anything frozen, put the fruit and vegetables together, the bottles and jars in one bag or box. This will save time and effort when unpacking at home and makes any delegating easily explained. Unpack and arrange everything in their appropriate places, and organize the refrigerator. Drinks and non-perishable vegetables tend to take up a lot of space, so pack them in cool-boxes if you have the space, or keep in the garage, shed or greenhouse if it is cold outside. Try to phone in any special orders well in advance and remember to pick them up!

Check the Basics

Go through your store cupboard, refrigerator and freezer and top up the basics – tea, coffee, sugar, flour, breakfast cereals, juice, eggs, milk, bread, butter. Don't forget everyday essentials like bin liners, kitchen roll and clingfilm, washing-up liquid, dishwasher powder, candles and matches, paper napkins, clean tea towels, aprons and so on. If it's summertime, clean out that barbecue and make sure you have enough fuel.

Easy Maintenance

As the weekend progresses, don't be tempted to let leftovers build up; they will take up valuable refrigerator space and you really won't use them. Keep on top of the washing up, and if not too worse for wear, try to set the breakfast table before you go to bed. If not, first up gets the task! This saves all that chaos caused by the 'grazing' habit.

Above all, if everyone helps out, the weekend will be a roaring success and the focus will be on enjoying and sharing each other's company.

ten golden rules of relaxed entertaining

Most people are too busy to entertain during the week. It's at the weekend that we have the time to enjoy ourselves. Drinks for a few friends, a dinner party, brunch or a long lunch in the garden – you might even have guests for the weekend. Apply these Golden Rules whenever you entertain – they're equally useful for small gatherings or large parties.

1

Planning the meals in advance will work miracles (and this includes breakfast). Keep it simple.

2

NEVER attempt to cook anything new when entertaining guests. Stick to what you know and are comfortable with – and do it well. If you have to, have a practice run on the family.

3

Always cook with ingredients that you can actually buy – if it's not in season or has to be bought from a Thai market two hours' drive away, think again or plan the shopping well in advance.

4

Check who eats what. If there is only one vegetarian among your guests, then plan a complete meal around that – if the food is good, then no one will notice. Asian food is a good choice.

5

Do as much of the shopping as possible in good time, making lists (sounds boring, but there's less chance of forgetting something). You can get real satisfaction from crossing things off the list.

6

If you aren't confident about your own cooking, make use of all the cooking short cuts and time-savers at your disposal. There are lots of reliable products out there, such as spice pastes (more aromatic than powders), ready-made pastry, or bases and mixes for homemade pizzas. Store-bought fresh custard diluted with a little liqueur can taste like real crème anglaise, and it will also take the fear out of making ice cream.

7

The store cupboard is the backbone of a busy person's kitchen. Keeping it well stocked means having everything you need to make an impromptu meal, rustle up a snack, or bake a batch of muffins in minutes. Ingredients in the store cupboard can lift an ordinary meal, add to a ready-prepared meal, or form the basis of an entire meal with just one or two fresh ingredients added.

8

Delegate or let others help; don't try to do it all yourself. Even if it's washing the dishes, setting the table or making drinks.

9

Make as much as you can in advance and store in the freezer. This will save hours, and having a well-stocked freezer is an entertaining security blanket. Things like soups, stews, ice cream, bread, butter and milk are handy standbys. Make notes to yourself on thawing times and when to take things out of the freezer.

10

ENJOY YOURSELF – don't make things difficult, just follow these rules. This will help your friends to relax as well. Entertaining your friends should be a pleasure.

party food

These delicious crisp biscuits are made in minutes. Store them uncooked in the freezer ready to pop into the oven at a moment's notice. Use 2 tablespoons olive oil instead of butter in the pastry for a lighter result.

parmesan and rosemary palmiers

50 g unsalted butter, softened

2 tablespoons chopped fresh rosemary

3 tablespoons freshly grated Parmesan cheese

2 sheets of ready-rolled frozen puff pastry, 20 cm square, thawed

coarse sea salt crystals

2 baking sheets, either non-stick or lined with baking parchment

Makes about 40

Mix the butter and rosemary together with half the Parmesan cheese. Spread thinly over the pastry squares.

Take one square of pastry and roll one edge in towards the middle. Roll the opposite edge in to meet the other one in the middle. Flip over until one roll is on top of the other. Flatten lightly with the palm of your hand. Repeat with the other square of pastry. Wrap the two rolls separately in clingfilm and chill or freeze until firm. When ready to bake, remove the clingfilm and cut each roll into about 20 slices.

Arrange on the baking sheets cut sides down, then sprinkle with the remaining Parmesan and a little coarse salt. Using a rolling pin, lightly roll the cheese and salt into the pastries.

Bake in a preheated oven at 220°C (425°F) Gas 7 for about 4 minutes on each side until risen and golden brown. Transfer to a wire rack to cool.

Alternatively, open-freeze, then pack in boxes. Bake from frozen in the same way, but for 2–3 minutes longer.

Use only perfectly ripe avocados for this – overripe ones will make the guacamole discolour quickly. To make it go further for larger numbers, stir in 150 ml sour cream – it will now serve 6–8 as a dip. Just double the quantities to serve more.

the best guacamole
with tortilla chips

2 large ripe avocados

freshly squeezed juice of 2 limes

1 small green chilli, deseeded and finely chopped

4 spring onions, very finely chopped

1 ripe medium tomato, skinned, deseeded and coarsely chopped

2–3 tablespoons coarsely chopped fresh coriander

sea salt and freshly ground black pepper

tortilla chips or crudités, to serve

Serves 4

Halve the avocados, remove the stones and scoop out the flesh into a bowl. Mash with a fork to give a coarse texture. Mix in half the lime juice, the chilli, spring onions, chopped tomato and coriander.

Taste and season with salt, pepper and more lime juice if necessary. Don't make this too far in advance because it will discolour quickly. Cover tightly with clingfilm, then stir well before serving. Serve with tortilla chips or crudités.

Avocado discoloration It is a myth that leaving an avocado stone in the finished dip will prevent discoloration. No matter what you do, it will discolour in the end. The only thing that works is adding enough lime juice and giving it a quick stir before you put it in the serving dish – and not making it too far in advance.

dukkah

No Egyptian home is complete without a jar of this wonderful seed and nut mixture in the larder. It is normally eaten as a snack – bread is dipped first into olive oil, then into the dukkah. I like to serve it with breadsticks and the most delicious olive oil I can find. It is also great used as a coating for chicken or fish instead of breadcrumbs.

150 g whole shelled hazelnuts

100 g whole shelled almonds

100 g sesame seeds

75 g coriander seeds

50 g ground cumin

1 teaspoon sea salt

½ teaspoon freshly ground black pepper

To serve

extra virgin olive oil

breadsticks or strips of toasted flatbread

Makes about 500 g

Put the hazelnuts, almonds and sesame seeds in an ovenproof dish in a preheated oven at 200°C (400°F) Gas 6 and toast for 5–10 minutes. Remove from the oven, then tip onto a plate to cool completely. If they aren't cool enough, they will turn oily when ground.

Toast the coriander seeds in a dry frying pan for 1–2 minutes until you can smell the aroma, tip onto the cooling nuts, then add the ground cumin to the pan. Toast for 30 seconds then transfer to the plate. When cold, put the nuts, spices, salt and pepper in a food processor and blend to a coarse, powdery meal – still dry-looking, but not totally pulverized. Spoon into a bowl and serve on a tray with a bowl of olive oil and the breadsticks.

oven-roasted spiced nuts

This recipe gives you control of the salt, the type of nut and the spice mix. When cool, mix in anything else you fancy, such as dried fruits or seeds.

40 g unsalted butter

1 tablespoon garam masala, Chinese five-spice, Cajun, or another spice mix, hot or mild

1 egg white

500 g mixed skinned nuts, such as almonds, Brazils, hazelnuts and pecans

1 teaspoon fine sea salt

Makes about 500 g

Melt the butter in a small saucepan and stir in the spices. Cool slightly, then whisk in the egg white until foamy. Add the nuts and toss well to coat. Spread the nuts out evenly in a thin layer in a roasting pan and roast slowly in a preheated oven at 150°C (300°F) Gas 2 for 30 minutes to 1 hour, stirring from time to time, until they are golden and toasted. Remove from the oven and toss the nuts with the salt.

Let cool completely, then store for at least 1 day (if you can wait) before eating. They will keep in an airtight tin for up to 2 weeks.

whole poached salmon
with sweet and sour pickled cucumber

1 large salmon, 1.5 kg, scaled and gutted through the gills if possible

Cucumber salad

2 large cucumbers
1 tablespoon sea salt
1 tablespoon caster sugar
100 ml white wine or cider vinegar
2 tablespoons chopped fresh dill
freshly ground white pepper

Court bouillon

1.5 litres water
1 tablespoon sea salt
150 ml white wine
1 onion, sliced
2 celery stalks, sliced
1 carrot, sliced
a handful of parsley stalks
2 bay leaves
1 teaspoon black peppercorns

To serve

extra chopped dill
thick homemade mayonnaise
wasabi paste (optional)

a fish kettle or large roasting tin and foil

Serves 6

There is something quite magnificent about serving a whole fish, simply decorated with pale green cucumber 'scales'. It is very impressive and so easy – my way of cooking the fish keeps it wonderfully moist, with no chance of overcooking or damaging the fish. A fish kettle is a good investment if you have regular access to fresh salmon and trout.

To make the cucumber salad, peel the cucumber and slice as thinly as possible with a mandoline or in a food processor. Spread in a colander and sprinkle with salt, mixing well. Stand the colander on a plate and leave to disgorge for 30 minutes. Rinse well and squeeze the excess moisture out of the cucumber. Spread the slices over a large plate. Dissolve the sugar in the vinegar and stir in the dill. Pour the mixture over the cucumber and let marinate for at least 1 hour before serving. Grind over lots of white pepper before serving with the salmon.

Put all the court bouillon ingredients in a large saucepan, bring to the boil and simmer for 1 hour. Let cool completely, then strain the liquid into a fish kettle. Lay the salmon on the rack of the fish kettle and lower into the liquid. The liquid must cover the fish; if not, top up with a little water. Bring slowly to the boil, then cover and turn off the heat. Let cool completely in the liquid. When completely cold, lift out and drain the fish, then remove the skin and slide onto a serving dish.

Cover the salmon with cucumber 'scales', serving any remaining cucumber separately. Sprinkle with dill and serve with thick homemade mayonnaise flavoured with a dash of Japanese wasabi paste, if using.

> **If serving hot,** bring the liquid to the boil, lower the heat to a bare simmer and poach the salmon for 4 minutes per 500 g. Remove the fish from the liquid, carefully pull off the skin and serve with melted butter or hollandaise.

We've had great fun cooking this in the open air over a wood fire, just as they do in Spain, but you can also use a portable gas burner. Paella is the perfect dish for outdoor parties – everything can be prepared ahead of time, then you just add the ingredients in a steady stream until the whole thing comes together. The smell is wonderfully enticing, so make enough for seconds.

a fabulous paella

3 tablespoons good olive oil

6 chicken thighs

175 g chorizo sausage, cut into chunks

2 garlic cloves, finely chopped

1 large onion, finely chopped

1 large red pepper, finely sliced

500 g Spanish paella rice

175 ml dry white wine

a good pinch of dried red chilli flakes

2 teaspoons sweet Spanish paprika

about 1.2 litres chicken stock

a large pinch of saffron strands, soaked in 3 tablespoons hot water

6 ripe tomatoes, quartered

12 whole uncooked prawns, in their shells

500 g fresh mussels, scrubbed, rinsed and debearded

125 g fresh or frozen peas

4 tablespoons chopped fresh flat leaf parsley

sea salt and freshly ground black pepper

wedges of lime or lemon, to serve

Serves 6

Heat the olive oil in a paella pan or large, deep frying pan. Add the chicken thighs and chorizo and brown all over, turning frequently. Stir in the garlic, onion and red pepper and cook for about 5 minutes until softened.

Stir in the rice until all the grains are coated and glossy. Add the wine and let it bubble and reduce until almost disappeared. Stir in the chilli flakes, paprika, chicken stock and soaked saffron. Stir well, bring to the boil and simmer gently for 10 minutes.

Stir in the tomatoes and prawns and cook gently for 5 minutes before finally tucking the mussels into the rice and adding the peas. Cook for another 5 minutes until the mussels open (take out any that do not open after this time). At this stage, almost all the liquid will have been absorbed and the rice will be tender.

Sprinkle the chopped parsley over the top and serve immediately, straight from the pan with a big pile of lime or lemon wedges on the side. This is messy food, so have plenty of paper napkins around.

Cooking mussels Live mussels keep well in a cool place (not the refrigerator), but you can also cook them beforehand. Clean them as described on page 63. Choose a large saucepan with a tight-fitting lid. Heat it dry, then tip in all the cleaned mussels. Add the wine, put on the lid and cook for about 5 minutes until the mussels open. Do not overcook and discard any that don't open. Drain in a colander set over a bowl, let cool and reserve both the mussels and their cooking liquid. (This can be done well in advance and chilled.) Add the mussel liquid to the paella at the same time as the wine, then add the mussels at the end to heat through.

This makes a beautiful centrepiece on a table – especially when arranged on a large platter. It needs nothing more than a cold noodle salad (page 98) to transform it into a feast for a summer party. Everything can be prepared ahead (even the day before) to be assembled at the last moment.

fillet of beef salad
with thai dressing

750 g piece beef fillet, from the thin end

2 tablespoons olive oil

175 g fine French beans, trimmed

3 large hard-boiled eggs

about 20 cm cucumber, peeled and cut into long wedges

250 g ripe tomatoes, quartered

75 g small wrinkled black olives

a handful of basil leaves, torn

sea salt and freshly ground black pepper

Beef marinade

2 tablespoons freshly squeezed lime juice

2 tablespoons olive oil

2 garlic cloves, crushed

Thai dressing

2 tablespoons fish sauce

3 tablespoons lime juice

2 tablespoons light soy sauce

1 tablespoon sweet chilli sauce

3 tablespoons chopped fresh coriander

Serves 4

To prepare the beef marinade, mix the lime juice, the 2 tablespoons olive oil, garlic, salt and pepper in a non-metal dish. Add the beef and toss to coat. Cover and let marinate in the refrigerator for 1 hour.

To cook the beef, heat another 2 tablespoons olive oil in a heavy roasting tin or frying pan on top of the stove until smoking. Lift the beef out of the marinade, pat dry and sear well all over until nicely browned. Transfer to a preheated oven at 200°C (400°F) Gas 6 and roast for 15–18 minutes for medium rare. Remove from the oven and transfer the beef to a plate to cool.

To make the dressing, put the fish sauce, lime juice, soy sauce, chilli sauce and coriander in a bowl, whisk well, then set aside to infuse.

Bring a saucepan of salted water to the boil, add the beans and blanch for 4 minutes. Drain, refresh in cold water, then set aside.

Peel the eggs and cut them in quarters. Heat the dressing and keep it warm. Toss the beans, cucumber, tomatoes and olives with half the dressing and pile on a flat serving platter.

Cut the beef in slices and lay them on top of the vegetables. Dot the eggs all around, strew with the basil, spoon over the remaining dressing and grind pepper on top before serving.

moroccan butterflied and barbecued lamb

2 kg leg of lamb, butterflied

1 tablespoon black peppercorns

1 tablespoon coriander seeds

1 tablespoon cumin seeds

1 tablespoon sweet paprika

2 teaspoon dried thyme

freshly squeezed juice of 1 lime

2 garlic cloves, crushed

100 ml plain yoghurt

sea salt

To serve

grilled flatbreads

salad

plain yoghurt mixed with chopped fresh mint

Serves 6–8

Moroccan lamb is one of the best and easiest meat dishes for a big barbecue party. Butterflied lamb is just a leg of lamb that has been split open and the bones removed so that it is flat and an even thickness. A butcher will do this for you, although it is quite easy to do yourself. After marinating, the leg can be cooked like one huge steak in much less time than cooking a whole leg, and is so easy to carve for large numbers.

Trim out any excess fat and score the meat where necessary to make it all the same thickness. Make deep slits all over the meat.

Put the peppercorns, coriander and cumin seeds and paprika in a dry frying pan, toast for a couple of minutes until aromatic, then grind or crush them. Transfer to a bowl, add the thyme, lime juice, garlic, yoghurt and salt to taste, then rub all over the cut side of the meat. Put in a shallow dish, cover and let marinate in the refrigerator for at least 1 hour.

To barbecue, cook the lamb skin side down over medium-hot coals for 10–12 minutes for medium rare, then turn it over and cook for a further 10–12 minutes. (For medium, cook for a total of 30–35 minutes, and for a total of 40 minutes for well done.)

To grill, put the lamb on a foil-lined rack under a medium-hot grill for 20 minutes, then turn it over and continue for a further 20 minutes (the meat should be medium).

When cooked, remove from the heat, cover loosely with foil and set aside in a warm place to rest for 10 minutes. Carve into long, thin slices. Serve with grilled pita breads, salad and minted yoghurt.

To butterfly a leg of lamb, find the place where the longest bone running down the length of the leg appears to be quite close to the skin. Using a small, sharp knife, slit through the thin surface along that bone and carefully peel the meat back from either side. Work around the bones at the thick end to release the meat, so it opens up like a book and you can lift them out. Open out the meat, skin side down – it should vaguely resemble the wings of a butterfly.

This hearty dish from south-west France is a firm family favourite. It is big and filling, and traditionally made with a type of haricot bean (lingots). However, I adore butter beans for their creamy texture, so that's what I use – feel free to differ. All the components of the dish can be made days in advance, then assembled on the day. It reheats very well (top up with a little more liquid if it looks dry) and is a boon for entertaining vast numbers without fuss. Make this for large gatherings on cold winter days.

a big pot of cassoulet

675 g dried butter beans, or other white beans

500 g smoked Italian pancetta, fat bacon or belly pork, in a piece

4 tablespoons olive oil

4 boneless duck breasts, halved crossways, or chicken legs or thighs

750 g fresh Toulouse sausages or Italian coarse pork sausages, cut into 3 pieces each

2 medium onions, chopped

1 large carrot, chopped

4–6 large garlic cloves, crushed

3 bay leaves

2 teaspoons dried thyme

2 whole cloves

3 tablespoons tomato purée

12 sun-dried tomatoes in oil, drained and coarsely chopped

75 g fresh white breadcrumbs (ciabatta is good too)

50 g butter

sea salt and freshly ground black pepper

Serves 6–8

The night before, put the beans in a very large bowl, cover with plenty of cold water (to cover them by their depth again) and let soak for several hours.

The next day, drain the beans well and tip into a large saucepan. Cover with fresh water, bring to the boil, then simmer for about 1 hour or until just cooked. Drain well (reserving the cooking liquid).

Trim and discard the rind from the pancetta, and cut the flesh into large pieces. Heat 2 tablespoons of the oil in a frying pan, brown the pieces in batches and transfer to a plate. Heat the remaining oil in the pan, add the duck breasts and fry skin side down until the skin is golden. Transfer to the same plate as the pancetta. Brown the sausages in the same way and add to the plate. Add the onions to the pan, then the carrot, garlic, bay leaves, dried thyme, cloves, tomato purée and sun-dried tomatoes. Cook for 5 minutes until softening.

To assemble the dish, put half the beans in a large, deep casserole. Add an even layer of all the meats, then the onion and tomato mixture. Season well with salt and pepper. Cover with the remaining beans, then add enough reserved hot cooking liquid until the beans are almost covered. Sprinkle evenly with breadcrumbs and dot with butter. Bake the cassoulet in a preheated oven at 180°C (350°F) Gas 4 for about 1 hour until a golden crust has formed. Serve warm straight out of the dish.

mexican pork and beans
in red chilli sauce

1 medium onion, coarsely chopped

4 garlic cloves, coarsely chopped

1 red pepper, halved, deseeded and coarsely chopped

1 fresh fat red chilli, deseeded and chopped

2 teaspoons mild chilli seasoning (powder)

1 teaspoon sweet paprika

1 teaspoon ground cumin

1 teaspoon coriander

½ teaspoon cinnamon

1 teaspoon dried oregano

300 ml lager beer

500 g pork or beef steak

4 tablespoons sunflower oil

400 g canned chopped tomatoes

350 ml tomato juice or passata (Italian puréed, sieved tomatoes)

25 g very dark chocolate, chopped

400 g canned pinto beans or black-eyed peas, drained and rinsed

sea salt and freshly ground black pepper

To serve

soft tortillas

tomato salsa

chopped avocado

sour cream

Green Rice (page 102)

Serves 4–6

This is my version of chili – not too spicy, made with pork, not beef, and just a few beans, then enriched Mexican-style with a little chocolate for depth. Serve it with generous bowls of a simple tomato, coriander and onion salsa, chopped cucumber in sour cream, a pile of warm tortillas and a big bowl of green rice for a great family feast. This is even better made the day before and it freezes very well. For vegetarians, leave out the meat and add cubed and roasted aubergines and quartered mushrooms.

Put the onion, garlic, red pepper, chilli, chilli seasoning, paprika, cumin, coriander, cinnamon and oregano in a blender or food processor. Add half the lager and blend to a smooth purée.

Trim the pork steaks, then cut into large pieces. Working in batches, heat the oil in a large saucepan, add the pork and fry until browned. Transfer to a plate.

Add the purée to the pan and cook, stirring continuously, over moderate heat for 5 minutes – make sure it doesn't catch and burn, but it should start to caramelize. Stir in the remaining lager, tomatoes, tomato juice, the pork and juices. Season with salt and pepper and bring to the boil. Reduce the heat and simmer very gently, half-covered, for 30–35 minutes until the pork is tender and the sauce thickened. Stir in the chocolate and beans and heat through.

Serve with the tortillas, salsa, avocado, sour cream and green rice.

Mild chilli seasoning is a mixture of chilli, cumin, salt, garlic powder and oregano and is a great all-purpose chilli powder for those who like spice but not too much heat.

brunch and
snacks

gorgeous granola

Packed with nutty goodness, this cereal is low in sugar and has no added salt. The best way to eat it is with a good dollop of yoghurt, a pile of blueberries and raspberries and some maple syrup. We should all being eating more seeds, nuts and grains and this mix knocks the spots off anything sold in health food shops. I have never liked breakfast cereals, but I can eat this in handfuls.

250 g rolled oats

125 g desiccated coconut

125 g chopped dried dates, cranberries or blueberries

125 g pumpkin seeds

125 g sunflower seeds

125 g sesame seeds

125 g linseed

125 g chopped pecans or almonds, macadamias, Brazils or other nuts

2 baking tins

Makes about 1.5 kg

Spread out the oats in the baking tins and toast in a preheated oven at 200°C (400°F) Gas 6 for 15–20 minutes, stirring frequently, until golden brown. Remove and let cool. Mix with all the other ingredients and store in an airtight container.

Variation For those who like to add sugar, stir 125 g soft brown sugar or 125 ml maple syrup into the oats before toasting. The sugar will melt onto the oats and give a crunch. The maple syrup will make the oats clump together in crunchy nodules.

overnight porridge

If you are lucky enough to have a slow-cooker or, even better, an Aga, then this is for you. Your breakfast will be waiting for you in the morning. Porridge cooked slowly overnight develops the flavour of the oatmeal and makes it really creamy. There's nothing better on a cold winter's morning to warm your tummy. I like to stir in fresh dates before eating. To make less, just adjust the ingredients, but the cooking time will be the same.

250 g pinhead or medium oatmeal (not porridge or rolled oats)

sea salt

cold milk or cream, honey and fruit, to serve (optional)

a slow-cooker (optional)

Serves 8

Just before going to bed, bring 1.75 litres cold water to the boil in a large saucepan. Add 2 teaspoons salt. Shower in the oatmeal, whisking all the time. Return to the boil and boil for 1 minute.

Either pour into a casserole, cover with the lid and put in a slow oven at 140°C (275°F) Gas 1 or the Aga. Alternatively, put the oatmeal mixture in the bowl of a preheated slow-cooker, cover with the lid and cook on LOW.

Cook for about 8 hours or overnight. The porridge will be ready the next day – you will have to remove a skin from the top and probably add a little boiling water to thin it down. Serve with cold milk or cream, honey and any fruit you like.

tea-infused fruit compote

Keep a big bowl of this compote in the refrigerator – it keeps well and is great with yoghurt and a sprinkling of seeds. With lighter teas, use lighter-flavoured fruits such as peaches and apples and flavour with lemon zest. Use orange zest to flavour stronger teas, together with stronger spices such as star anise. There is no need to add sugar, because the natural sugars from the fruits thicken the syrup as it cooks.

2 teaspoons leaf tea, such as Earl Grey, jasmine or other tea

500 g mixed dried fruit, such as prunes, apricots, figs or others

300 ml apple juice

2 crushed cardamom pods

1 cinnamon stick

thinly peeled zest of 1 unwaxed orange

Serves 4

Make a large pot of tea with the leaf tea and 1 litre boiling water and set aside to brew. Put the fruit in a bowl and completely cover with the brewed tea. Cover and let soak for several hours or overnight.

Transfer to a saucepan, then add the apple juice, cardamom pods, cinnamon stick and orange zest. Bring slowly to the boil, then reduce the heat and simmer for about 20 minutes until soft. Remove all the spices and let cool.

Cover and chill in the refrigerator. This will keep for a week in the refrigerator, and can be frozen.

swiss muesli

After tasting this on a skiing holiday in Switzerland, I can't think why anyone would eat dried muesli again. Soaking the oats in apple juice (or other juice) overnight transforms them from dry and dusty to light and flavoursome. The finer the oats, the smoother the texture. Delicious with creamy plain yoghurt stirred in.

about 200 ml measured porridge oats, rolled oats or oat flakes

200 g large raisins or other dried fruit

600 ml apple juice

600 ml plain yoghurt

4 apples, grated or chopped

4 bananas or a mixture of seasonal fruit

4 oranges, peeled and segmented or chopped

clear honey, to taste

Makes 4 large portions

Put the oats and raisins in a bowl and pour over the apple juice. Cover and let soak in the refrigerator overnight.

The next day, stir in the yoghurt, then add more fruit juice and honey to taste. Stir in half the fruit and sprinkle the remaining fruit on top.

bacon and eggs in a pan

A whole breakfast made without fuss in one pan. Use the best bacon you can find and fresh free-range eggs. It's made like a giant omelette – a British version of Italian frittata. Serve in wedges.

1 tablespoon sunflower oil

8 slices dry cure back bacon

6 large eggs

10 cherry tomatoes, halved

2 tablespoons scissor-snipped fresh chives

sea salt and freshly ground black pepper

Serves 4

Heat a large, preferably non-stick frying pan, about 27 cm diameter, over medium heat. Add 1 tablespoon sunflower oil, heat, then add the bacon. Cook for 2 minutes until it is beginning to brown and crisp around the edges.

Break the eggs into a bowl, add salt and pepper and whisk lightly. Pour into the pan around the bacon, making sure the base is covered and the bacon sits half-submerged. Dot with the tomatoes and cook over medium to low heat until the eggs have set. Sprinkle with chives and serve immediately, cut into wedges.

fearless scrambled eggs

Scrambled eggs should be lovely and creamy, not watery grey lumps. You cannot make these in advance, just wait until everyone is around and cook them in seconds. I use a non-stick saucepan and a spurtle (wooden porridge stirrer, often with a thistle handle), but a wooden spoon or spatula will do. Eat them as soon as they are cooked – they do not hang around.

6 large very fresh free-range eggs

3 tablespoons milk or cream

50 g unsalted butter

3 tablespoons chopped fresh parsley

sea salt and freshly ground black pepper

buttered toasted English muffins, to serve

Serves 4

Put the eggs, milk and a pinch of salt and pepper in a bowl and whisk until smooth. Melt the butter in a non-stick saucepan until foaming. Pour in the eggs and cook over medium heat until they start to set on the base of the pan (use the spoon to scrape the bottom to check). Cook them, stirring slowly but constantly, and scraping the bottom and sides of the pan to mix in the cooking eggs. Continue scraping, mixing and stirring, until the eggs thicken and start to look like lumpy but creamy custard. Taste and season and stir in the parsley. Spoon onto buttered, toasted muffins and serve immediately.

Variations

• Stir in chopped smoked salmon or other smoked fish just before the eggs are ready.

• Cook 3 chopped spring onions in the butter, add a little chopped fresh ginger and a little chopped fresh chilli. Stir in ½ teaspoon curry powder and a couple of chopped tomatoes and cook until soft. Add the eggs and cook as above, stirring in 2 tablespoons chopped fresh coriander at the last moment.

sausage and bacon rolls

There's nothing quite like a warm sausage-filled roll for brunch. Dotting the sausages with mustard and wrapping them in bacon just adds to the taste experience and the cooking smells will waken even the most hung-over. Get these under way while you make juice and tea or coffee.

16 thin slices Italian pancetta or streaky bacon

a little mustard (any kind)

8 all-meat butcher's sausages

olive oil, for brushing

To serve

4 warm buttered soft rolls or even small naan bread or pita bread

tomato ketchup or grilled tomatoes

Serves 4

Preheat the grill to medium. Spread a little mustard over each slice of bacon. Wrap 2 slices around each sausage. Put the sausages on the rack of a grilling pan so that the loose ends of the bacon are underneath the sausage. Brush with a little oil and grill for about 6–8 minutes on each side, depending on the thickness of the sausage, until the bacon is crisp and the sausage cooked through. Serve in buttered rolls with plenty of ketchup or grilled tomatoes.

nut butter on toast

Homemade nut butter is SO much better than bought peanut butter, and most impressive, taking seconds to make. You can use blanched nuts, but I like to leave the skins on. You can mix two or three varieties together for a more sophisticated taste, but make sure they are very fresh – stale nuts will make nasty butter. If too rich, you can add a few tablespoons tahini paste to the nuts before grinding.

500 ml sunflower oil

125 g shelled nuts, such as Brazils, cashews, almonds, hazelnuts or walnuts

a pinch of sea salt

Makes about 600 ml

Pour the oil into a blender or food processor with a sharp blade (a blender will give a smoother result). Add the nuts and a pinch of salt. Pulse in short bursts, scraping down the sides every now and then to make it blend evenly. Taste, adding extra salt if necessary. Pack into screwtop jars and store in a cold place or in the refrigerator.

Use this basic mix to create different kinds of flavoured muffins. If you prepare the dry mix the day before, you can quickly rustle up some muffins first thing in the morning.

muffin mania

250 g plain flour

125 g caster sugar

1 tablespoon baking powder

½ teaspoon sea salt

1 large egg

125 ml milk (or a little more)

50 ml sunflower oil

a 6- or 12-hole muffin tin, greased with butter

paper cases (see tip)

Makes 12 small or 6 large muffins

Preheat the oven to 180°C (350°F) Gas 4. Sift the flour, sugar, baking powder and salt together into a large bowl or plastic bag.

Whisk the egg in a large bowl, then whisk in the milk and oil. Add the dry ingredients and stir until just blended. The mixture should look very coarse with lumps and floury pockets.

Spoon into the prepared muffin tin, filling three-quarters full. Bake for about 20 minutes or until well risen and golden brown.

Remove from the oven and turn the tray upside down onto a cooling rack. Leave for 2 minutes for the steam to loosen the muffins. Lift off the tray and turn the muffins the right way up. Serve warm – they do not reheat well.

Variations
• Experiment with different flours, and adjust the liquid accordingly because wholemeal flours tend to absorb more liquid.
• Add nuts, seeds and dried fruits to the basic mixture.
• Use soft brown sugar instead of caster sugar.
• Sift in spices with the dry ingredients.
• Quickly stir whole berries or chopped fresh fruit into the mix before baking.
• For a crunchy topping, mix chopped nuts and seeds into soft brown sugar and sprinkle on top of the muffins before baking.

Tip Put a paper case in each muffin cup and they will never stick.

soups and starters

This isn't so difficult to make – and very impressive. I like to use smoked salmon fillet for this (sometimes known as royal fillet). It is very meaty and you can cut it to the size you want. It may not be truly authentic, but it is great served with drinks on a hot summer's night. The uncut rolls can be wrapped up tightly in clingfilm, then cut and unwrapped at the last moment to preserve the freshness.

smoked salmon and cucumber sushi rolls

375 g Japanese sushi rice

2 tablespoons caster sugar

1 teaspoon sea salt

4 tablespoons rice wine vinegar

1 large cucumber, unwaxed if possible

5 sheets dried nori seaweed

200 g sliced smoked salmon

3 teaspoons wasabi paste

To serve

Japanese pickled ginger

Japanese soy sauce, such as tamari

wasabi paste

a sushi mat or a clean cloth

Serves 6

Put the rice in a sieve and wash well under running water until the water runs clear. Drain well and tip into a saucepan. Add 600 ml water and bring to the boil. Boil fast for 5 minutes, reduce the heat, cover and cook slowly for 10 minutes until all the water has been absorbed.

Meanwhile, put the sugar, salt and vinegar in a bowl and stir until dissolved. Tip the cooked rice onto a plate or tray and sprinkle with the vinegar mixture. Mix lightly with your hands, then let cool.

Cut the cucumber into strips the length of the long side of the nori.

To make the sushi rolls, put a sheet of nori shiny side down on a sushi mat or clean cloth. Spread one-fifth of the rice over the nori, leaving a clear strip down one long edge. Cover the rice with a thin layer of smoked salmon and spread with a little wasabi paste (thin it down with a little water if you like). Put a cucumber strip along the side opposite the clear strip of seaweed. Dampen the clear end. Starting from the cucumber end, and using the mat to help you, roll up like a Swiss roll, sealing it into a secure cylinder with the dampened edge.

Using a very sharp knife, cut into 2 cm lengths. Repeat with the remaining seaweed, rice and salmon. Serve with pickled ginger, soy sauce and more wasabi for dipping.

These small, spicy, savoury jellies are served in glasses with rich and salty tapenade spread on thin toasts. There's a surprise olive hidden in the centre of each jelly, but you could always substitute a lightly boiled quail's egg instead.

jellied bloody marys
with tapenade toasts

1 sachet powdered gelatine, 11.7 g

600 ml tomato juice

150 ml vodka

freshly squeezed juice of 2 limes or 1 lemon

1 tablespoon Worcestershire sauce

1 teaspoon Tabasco sauce

freshly ground black pepper

celery salt

Quick tapenade

175 g Greek-style black olives, pitted, plus 6 extra to serve

2 garlic cloves, peeled

3 canned anchovy fillets, drained

2 teaspoons capers, drained

1 tablespoon olive oil, plus extra for the jar

1 small baguette loaf, to serve

Serves 6

Put 3 tablespoons water in a very small saucepan, sprinkle with the gelatine and leave to swell and sponge. Heat gently to dissolve.

Put the tomato juice, vodka, strained lemon juice, Worcestershire and Tabasco sauces in a jug, season generously with black pepper and celery salt and mix well. Stir in the melted gelatine, mix well and pour into 6 glasses set on a tray until half full. Refrigerate for 30 minutes until set, but keep the remaining jelly out of the refrigerator to stay liquid.

Put an olive on top of each set jelly, spoon over a little liquid jelly, then refrigerate to set and anchor the olive. Finally, fill with the remaining jelly and chill until set and ready to serve.

Meanwhile, to make the tapenade, put the olives, garlic, anchovies, capers and olive oil in a food processor and blend until smooth. Scrape out into a jar and cover with a layer of olive oil until needed. Cut the baguette into very thin slices and toast on both sides until golden. Spread thinly with the tapenade.

Put a glass of jelly on each plate with a pile of toasts and serve immediately.

This is one of those simple, stunning dishes that is divine and addictive. You pull the garlic apart with your fingers and squeeze the golden purée onto each mouthful of bruschetta as you go. Try to use goats' cheese with a rind because it will help contain the cheese while it's melting under the grill.

grilled goats' cheese and rosemary bruschetta
with baked garlic cloves

4 thick slices country bread, preferably sourdough

2 garlic cloves, peeled and bruised

extra virgin olive oil

4 tablespoons basil pesto (page 64)

8 thick slices goats' cheese with rind, such as Boucheron chèvre

sea salt and freshly ground black pepper

Baked garlic

4 large heads of garlic

175 ml olive oil, heated

4 sprigs of thyme

2–3 sprigs of rosemary

sea salt and freshly ground black pepper

Serves 4

To prepare the garlic, slice off the top third of each bulb. Pack cut side up in a small baking dish, pour over the olive oil and tuck in the thyme and a couple of rosemary sprigs. Season well with salt and pepper and bake in a preheated oven at 160°C (325°F) Gas 3 for about 1 hour until meltingly soft.

Remove the garlic from the oven and let cool until warm.

Meanwhile, barbecue, toast or pan-grill the bread on one side only until lightly charred or browned, rub each cooked side with the bruised garlic, then sprinkle with oil. Keep warm.

Spread the pesto over the ungrilled side of the bruschetta and put 2 slices of cheese on each one. Sprinkle with salt and pepper and cook under a hot grill for 1–2 minutes or until the cheese is beginning to melt and colour (watch that the bread doesn't catch and burn).

Pull the garlic cloves apart and serve a few cloves on top of each bruschetta with a little more oil. Squeeze out the soft garlic and spread onto the bruschetta, then serve.

Normally this dish is made from aubergines that have been roasted whole and the flesh scooped out. In this version, I peel them first, then slice and roast in the oven, so the result is much more mellow. This creamy dip can be part of a selection of meze dishes served as an informal starter.

baba ghanoush

1 kg aubergines

about 150 ml olive oil

2 garlic cloves, crushed

4 tablespoons tahini (sesame seed paste)

freshly squeezed juice of 1–2 lemons, or to taste

sea salt and freshly ground black pepper

To serve

1 tablespoon sweet paprika

3 tablespoons olive oil

2 tablespoon chopped fresh flat leaf parsley

pita bread or other flatbread

a baking sheet

Serves 4–6

Trim the aubergines, peel, then slice thickly. Arrange the pieces on a baking sheet and brush both sides with olive oil. Roast in a preheated oven at 200°C (400°F) Gas 6 for about 20 minutes until browning and soft, turning them at least once.

Remove from the oven and let cool for 5 minutes. Transfer to a food processor and add the garlic, tahini and the juice of 1 lemon. Process until creamy, then taste and adjust the seasoning with salt, pepper and more lemon juice.

Pour or spoon into a shallow dish. Mix the paprika with the 3 tablespoons olive oil and trickle it over the top of the baba ghanoush. Sprinkle with parsley and serve with pita bread for dipping.

Note For a softer garlic flavour, roast the garlic cloves whole and unpeeled with the aubergines, then squeeze the soft flesh out of the skins and blend with the aubergines.

To cook aubergines in the microwave, prick 2 medium aubergines all over with the point of a sharp knife. This will stop them exploding in the oven. Line the turntable of the microwave with a double layer of kitchen paper and put the aubergines on top. Microwave on HIGH for about 12 minutes (for 500 g) or until collapsed and completely soft. Cut open and scoop out the flesh. This will make a lighter, sharper dip.

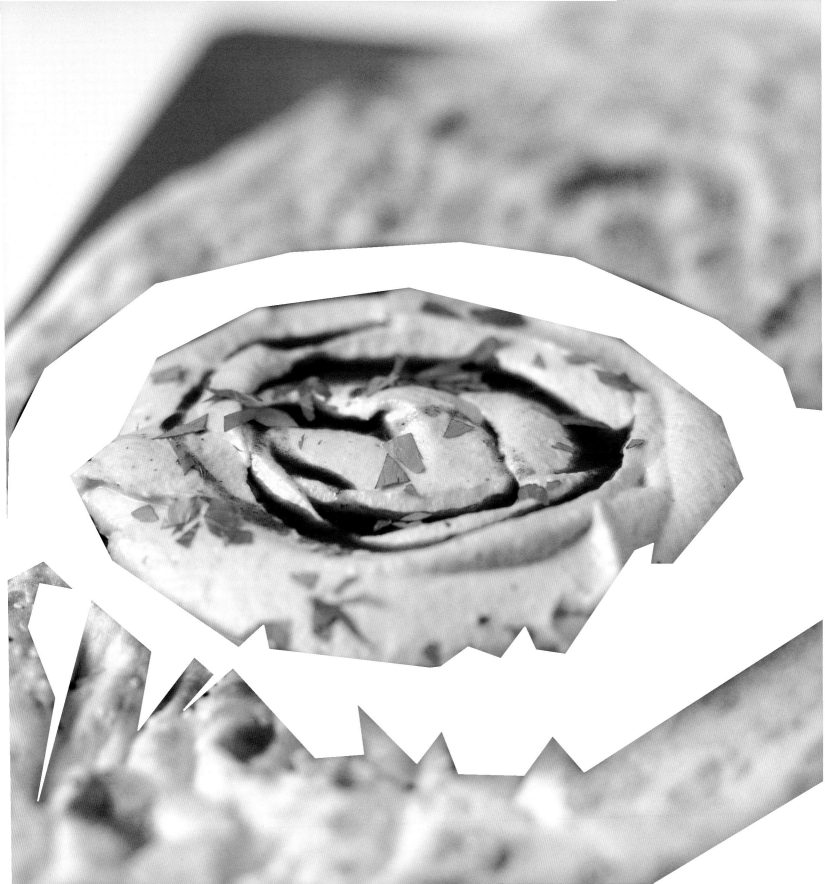

This exceptionally smooth, creamy pâté makes an impressive starter, especially when served with toasted brioche and a sharp fruity chutney to cut the richness. The parfait can also be set in individual pots, and I would pour a layer of melted unsalted butter on top to seal them.

chicken liver parfait
with bitter orange and onion chutney

500 g chicken livers, fresh or frozen and thawed

150 g butter, softened

2 shallots, peeled and finely chopped

90 ml cognac, Armagnac or Madeira

90 ml double cream or crème fraîche

a large pinch of ground mace

a large pinch of allspice

sea salt and freshly ground black pepper

warm toasted brioche or char-grilled bread, to serve

Bitter orange and onion chutney

3 unwaxed oranges

400 g red onions, peeled and chopped

150 g cooking apples, peeled, cored and chopped

200 g chunky dark marmalade

100 g dark muscovado sugar

300 ml cider or white wine vinegar

sea salt and freshly ground black pepper

a 450 g loaf tin, lined with clingfilm

Serves 4–6: makes 600 ml chutney

Trim the chicken livers, discarding any white fibrous parts and discoloured bits.

Melt 25 g butter in a frying pan, add the shallots and cook gently for 1–2 minutes until beginning to soften. Increase the heat slightly and add the livers. Turn them in the pan for 2–3 minutes until just browned and 'seized', but still soft and pink on the inside. Tip into a blender. Deglaze the pan with the cognac, scraping up any sediment. Boil to reduce by half, then add to the blender. Add the cream, plenty of salt and pepper, then the mace and allspice. Blend until smooth. Add the remaining butter and blend again until smooth. Push the mixture through a sieve and check the seasoning. Spoon into the prepared tin and level the surface. Cool, then refrigerate for several hours or overnight until firm.

Meanwhile, to make the chutney, peel the oranges. Finely shred or chop the rind of 1 orange and discard the remaining rind. Chop the flesh of the oranges and put into a non-reactive saucepan. Add the onions, apples, marmalade, sugar, vinegar, salt and pepper. Bring to the boil, then simmer for about 1 hour, stirring every now and then until very thick and pulpy. Spoon into a jar, seal and cool. This will keep in the refrigerator for at least a month.

To serve, turn out the parfait, remove the clingfilm and cut into slices with a warm knife. Serve with warm toasted brioche or char-grilled bread and some chutney.

700 g fresh ripe tomatoes, cored and quartered

300 ml tomato or V8 juice

1 small garlic clove, peeled and crushed

1 medium red pepper, halved,
deseeded and coarsely chopped

2 spring onions, trimmed and coarsely chopped

1 cucumber, peeled and coarsely chopped

2 tablespoons chopped fresh coriander

2 tablespoons sherry vinegar

1 tablespoon sweet chilli sauce

sea salt and freshly ground black pepper

Frozen vegetable cubes

3 tablespoons finely chopped cucumber

3 tablespoons finely chopped red pepper

3 tablespoons finely chopped radishes

3 tablespoons finely chopped tomato

Serves 6

I add jewel-like cubes of frozen finely chopped vegetables
to the soup instead of the usual blocks of watery ice cubes.

jewelled gazpacho

Put the tomatoes and juice in a blender and blend until smooth. Pour half
into a jug. Mix all the remaining vegetables in a bowl. Add half the vegetables
to the blender, blend again until smooth and transfer to a bowl. Put the
tomato mixture, the remaining vegetables and the coriander in the blender,
blend until smooth, then add to the bowl. Stir well, then mix in the
vinegar, chilli sauce and salt and pepper to taste. Cover and chill overnight.

To make the frozen vegetable cubes, mix the chopped vegetables
together and pack into ice-cube trays. Freeze.

Ladle the soup into chilled bowls or tumblers and put a couple of frozen
vegetable cubes in each one.

This is a gorgeously smooth and velvety soup that will suit all tastes and any occasion, from picnics to dinner parties. To ensure a really smooth texture, it is very important to blend, then sieve the soup before serving hot or chilled.

leek and potato soup
with watercress purée

75 g unsalted butter

2 medium onions, thinly sliced

500 g leeks (white part only), thinly sliced

175 g floury potatoes, chopped

1.35 litres chicken stock

300 ml milk

150 ml crème fraîche, plus extra to serve

sea salt and freshly ground white pepper

Watercress purée

125 g watercress, washed

5 tablespoons good olive oil

Serves 6

To make the purée, pick the leaves off the watercress stalks and put in a blender with the olive oil. Blend until smooth. Pour into a screwtop jar and set aside.

To make the soup, melt the butter in a large saucepan and add the onions and leeks. Stir well, add 3 tablespoons water, cover tightly and cook over gentle heat for 10 minutes until soft and golden, but not at all brown.

Stir in the potatoes and chicken stock. Bring to the boil, reduce the heat, cover and simmer for 20 minutes until the potatoes are tender. Stir in the milk, then purée in a blender or with a hand-held stick blender. Press the purée through a sieve, then return it to the pan. Stir in the crème fraîche and season with salt and pepper to taste. Cool and chill (if serving chilled, add extra seasoning) or serve hot in warm soup bowls with a swirl of watercress purée and dollop of chilled crème fraîche.

chickpea chermoula soup

400 g dried chickpeas, soaked overnight in water with a pinch of bicarbonate of soda, or 800 g canned chickpeas, drained and rinsed

50 g unsalted butter or 3 tablespoons olive oil, plus extra to serve

100 g Italian pancetta, lardons or streaky bacon, chopped (optional)

2 medium onions, finely chopped

1 carrot, chopped

1 celery stalk, chopped

2 garlic cloves, finely chopped

½ teaspoon sweet paprika

½ teaspoon ground cinnamon

½ teaspoon ground ginger

½ teaspoon ground cumin

½ teaspoon dried thyme

400 g canned chopped tomatoes

150 g prepared baby spinach leaves

50 g chopped fresh coriander

sea salt and freshly ground black pepper

Serves 6

Drain the chickpeas, put in a saucepan, cover with fresh water and bring to the boil. Cover and simmer for 40 minutes or until tender. Alternatively, used canned chickpeas for a quick version.

Meanwhile, heat the butter in a frying pan, and add the pancetta or bacon if using. Fry over medium heat until the fat begins to run. Add the chopped vegetables and garlic and cook for 5–10 minutes until beginning to soften and brown. Stir in the spices and thyme and cook for 1 minute. When cooked, drain the chickpeas, reserve the cooking liquid and return the pulses to the pan. Stir in the pancetta and vegetables, the tomatoes and about 1 litre reserved cooking liquid to cover completely. Bring to the boil, half-cover, reduce the heat and simmer for 30 minutes, stirring occasionally. The chickpeas should start to disintegrate and thicken the soup. Add salt and pepper to taste, then stir in the spinach and coriander 5 minutes before serving sprinkled with olive oil.

fiery red pepper soup

If making this for children, omit the chillies and use 500 ml milk mixed with 500 ml stock.

6 medium red peppers

375 g carrots

1–2 fresh red chillies

750 g ripe plum tomatoes

3 large garlic cloves, peeled

6 tablespoons olive oil

2 teaspoons smoked sweet paprika (Spanish pimentón dulce)

1.2 litres vegetable or beef stock

sea salt and freshly ground black pepper

crisply fried bacon slices, to serve

Makes 2.2 litres: serves 8

Cut the stalk ends off the peppers, halve and scrape out the seeds. Scrape the carrots and cut into chunky fingers.

If using chillies, cut off the stalks, cut in half and scrape out the seeds (using rubber gloves if you like).

Put the peppers, carrots, chillies, tomatoes and garlic in large roasting tins so the vegetables aren't too cramped, then toss them in the olive oil. Season well with salt and pepper. Roast in a preheated oven at 200°C (400°F) Gas 6 for about 30 minutes until all the vegetables are soft and slightly charred at the edges.

Transfer half the vegetables to a blender, add the paprika and half the stock and blend until smooth. Pour into a saucepan and repeat with the remaining vegetables and stock, adding extra stock if it seems too thick. Reheat until almost boiling, add salt and pepper to taste, then serve with the bacon crumbled over the top.

main dishes

Make your own Green Thai Curry Paste (page 136) and keep it in the refrigerator for the best flavour, or buy some the next time you visit an Oriental store – they keep well.

green prawn curry
with thin noodles

1 litre fish or vegetable stock

4 tablespoons Green Thai Curry Paste (page 136)

250 g (4 nests) stir-fry thin rice noodles

400 g canned coconut milk

750 g uncooked peeled prawns or tofu

125 g frozen peas

3 tablespoons chopped fresh coriander

sea salt

To serve

6 spring onions, shredded

1 red pepper, halved, deseeded and finely shredded

Serves 6

Put 250 ml of the stock and all the curry paste in a sauté pan, whisk well, then bring to the boil. Simmer for 2 minutes until all the liquid has evaporated. Add the remaining stock and stir well. Bring to the boil, reduce the heat and simmer for 10 minutes.

Meanwhile bring a large saucepan of water to the boil, add the noodles, cover, remove from the heat and let soak for 4 minutes. Stir, then drain well.

Pour the coconut milk into the curry sauce, add the prawns and peas, stir well and simmer for 5 minutes. Stir in the noodles and chopped coriander, taste and season with salt. Serve topped with shredded spring onions and red pepper.

If using tofu, cut into large cubes and fry on one side for 2 minutes in very hot oil in a non-stick frying pan. Turn the pieces over and cook for a further 2 minutes. Add to the curry at the last moment.

I have happy memories of a mussel feast my sister and I cooked for twelve friends many years ago. Everyone pitched in. Lots of willing hands helped to scrub the mussels. We set up a trestle table and covered it with a large white bedsheet tablecloth. While the mussels were cooking (and it took some time for such a large volume), the bread was warmed, and much wine flowed. We had borrowed a huge catering pot from a friend and it had to be stirred occasionally by the strongest and bravest. It was one of the best meals I have ever had and it went on for hours. Take the pot to the table and ladle out the mussels first, then serve the delicious soupy juices to be mopped up with crusty bread.

moules marinière feast

3 kg fresh mussels

4 tablespoons olive oil

3 garlic cloves, very finely chopped

3 onions, very finely chopped

200 ml dry white wine

a good pinch of chilli flakes

4 tablespoons coarsely chopped fresh flat leaf parsley

To serve

lemon wedges

lots of hot French bread

a large piece of muslin

Serves 6

Scrub the mussels well, knock off any barnacles and pull off the beards. Discard any broken mussels and any that won't close when they are tapped on the work surface. Drain in a colander.

Heat the oil in a large saucepan. Add the garlic and onions and fry for 10 minutes until softened but not coloured. Add the wine, chilli flakes and 200 ml water, bring to the boil and simmer for another 10 minutes. (This can be done in advance.) Add the mussels, cover and cook over high heat for about 5 minutes, shaking the pan every now and then, until the mussels have opened. Discard any that remain closed. Strain the mussels through a muslin-lined colander set over a bowl or saucepan.

Keep the mussels warm in the colander and boil the mussel liquid to reduce slightly. Stir in the chopped parsley. Pile the mussels into warmed bowls, and pour over the hot broth. Serve with lemon wedges and the bread to mop up the broth.

Marinating salmon concentrates the flavour and gives the steaks a lovely glaze when grilled. Melted pesto makes a wonderful sauce – add more olive oil if you like it thinner and less rich. Although cherry or baby plum tomatoes look and taste great, you can use larger ones chopped to a similar size – just make sure they are properly ripe.

salmon steaks
with hot pesto and tomatoes

4 salmon steaks, 175 g each

2 tablespoons balsamic vinegar

2 teaspoons soy sauce

350 g baby plum tomatoes, halved

extra basil leaves, to serve

Basil pesto

2 garlic cloves, peeled

55 g pine nuts

4 tablespoons freshly grated Parmesan
or aged pecorino cheese

55 g fresh basil leaves (no stalks)

150 ml extra virgin olive oil

55 g unsalted butter, softened

sea salt and freshly ground black pepper

Serves 4

Put the salmon in a shallow non-metallic dish. Put the balsamic vinegar and soy sauce in a measuring jug, mix well, then pour over the steaks, turning to coat. Cover and let marinate in the refrigerator for 30 minutes.

To make the pesto, put everything in a blender or food processor and blend until as smooth as you like. Store in a jar with a layer of olive oil on top to exclude the air. Keep in the refrigerator until needed, making sure that each time you use it, you level the surface and re-cover with olive oil.

Remove the salmon from the marinade and put in a foil-lined pan. Cook under a preheated grill for 4 minutes on each side, brushing with the marinade once on each side. Remove from the grill and keep warm. Put the pesto in a saucepan and heat gently until warm and melted. Carefully stir in the tomatoes. Serve the salmon on warm plates with the pesto tomato sauce spooned over, then topped with basil.

Pesto freezes well, so when the best basil is around in the summer, I make and freeze pesto in ice-cube trays, then pop the cubes out into plastic bags. Don't thaw the cubes, just let them melt into whatever's cooking.

If your tomatoes aren't ripe enough, put them on a sunny windowsill or in the fruit bowl for 2–3 days – they will completely change. The refrigerator is death to a tomato.

chicken with forty cloves of garlic

2 kg free-range organic chicken

2 lemons, sliced

4 sprigs of thyme

a few large sprigs of rosemary

a few sprigs of sage

5 bay leaves

200 ml olive oil

40 unpeeled fat garlic cloves

500 g plain flour

sea salt and freshly ground black pepper

12 thin croûtes or toasts, to serve

Serves 4

A great alternative to The Sunday Roast. It's a classic dish from Provence, using all the herby flavours of the hot sunny hillside, olive oil and of course a massive amount of garlic. The long cooking makes the garlic meltingly tender. The chicken is carved and served with the garlic, which is then squeezed out of the skins and spread onto crisp toasts.

Season the cavity of the bird with salt and pepper. Add the sliced lemon and 2 sprigs of thyme. Push 2 sprigs of thyme, 2 sprigs of rosemary, 2 sprigs of sage and 2 bay leaves between the skin and the breast on both sides of the chicken. Pour the olive oil into a casserole and turn the chicken around in it to coat it all over. Add the garlic cloves and remaining herbs and mix with the oil to coat. Sprinkle with salt and pepper.

Mix the flour with enough water to make into a soft dough. Roll the dough into a long cylinder and press it around the edge of the casserole. Push the lid down on top and press any overhanging dough up and over the edge of the lid to seal.

Bake in a preheated oven at 180°C (350°F) Gas 4 for 1½ hours. By this time, the chicken will be cooked, but will happily sit unopened for 15–20 minutes. Take the dish to the table, crack open the crust and lift off the lid to release the aroma of Provence.

Carve or joint the chicken and serve each portion with the collected juices and a pile of garlic to spread on toasts.

All the flavours of the Tuscan hillside are captured in these little parcels. Rosemary and sage grow wild there, and are the most common used in Tuscan cooking. Don't be alarmed at the amount of salt and pepper used – this gives it the authentic punchy flavour. A great dish to prepare ahead and cook at the last moment.

chicken with tuscan herbs

4 garlic cloves

2 teaspoons sea salt

1 teaspoon freshly ground black pepper

3 tablespoons chopped fresh
rosemary and sage, mixed

12 boneless skinless free-range chicken thighs

24 black Greek-style olives, stoned and chopped

12 thin slices pancetta or streaky bacon

12 fresh bay leaves

To serve

olive oil

Olive Oil and Parmesan Mash (see note)

kitchen string

Serves 6

Pound the garlic, salt, pepper and rosemary with a mortar and pestle. Rub the paste generously all over the flesh side of the thighs. Dot with the olives. Reshape the thighs and wrap each one with a slice of pancetta and tuck in a bay leaf. Tie each parcel in 2 places with fine string. (They can be frozen at this stage – remove from the freezer and thaw at room temperature for 2 hours before cooking.)

Arrange the parcels on a grilling pan and brush with olive oil. Cook under a preheated grill for 20 minutes, turning every 5 minutes until golden and crisp and cooked through. Alternatively, bake in a preheated oven at 200°C (400°F) Gas 6 for 20–25 minutes. Sprinkle with extra olive oil and serve with olive oil and Parmesan mash.

Note Olive Oil and Parmesan Mash
Make the basic recipe for Perfect Mashed Potatoes on page 102. Heat 4 tablespoons of olive oil with the milk instead of the butter, then beat in 55 g freshly grated Parmesan.

The fillet is the most tender cut of beef and is best cooked until rosy pink inside. Resting the meat before carving will ensure a juicy result.

perfect roast fillet of beef
with herbed yorkshire puddings

1 kg whole fillet of beef (not from the thick end)

olive oil

sea salt and freshly ground black pepper

200 g thinly sliced pancetta or thinly sliced dry-cure streaky bacon

Herbed Yorkshire puddings

225 g plain white flour

½ teaspoon salt

2 large sprigs of rosemary, chopped

1 tablespoon chopped fresh thyme

4 eggs

600 ml milk

8 tablespoons beef dripping, duck fat or vegetable oil

To serve

Vichy Carrots (page 105)

Spring Onion and Horseradish Mash (page 102)

kitchen string

a 12-hole muffin tin or Yorkshire pudding tin

Serves 6

To make the Yorkshire puddings, sift the flour and salt into a food processor or blender. Add the rosemary and thyme, eggs and milk. Blend until smooth and pour into a jug. Cover and refrigerate for at least 1 hour.

Trim the fillet of all fat and membrane and neatly tie at regular intervals to give a good shape. Rub all over with olive oil, salt and pepper. Wrap with the pancetta. Cover and set aside for 20 minutes at room temperature.

Put the meat in a roasting tin and cook in a preheated oven at 230°C (450°F) Gas 8 for 25 minutes for medium rare (20 for very rare, 35 for medium). Remove from the oven, cover loosely with foil and let rest in a warm place for 10–15 minutes (this will make it easier to carve and give the meat an even pink colour).

Lower the oven temperature to 200°C (400°F) Gas 6 and cook the puddings while the meat is resting. Put the dripping into the holes of the muffin tin and heat in the oven for a couple of minutes. Stir the batter and pour into the hot pans – it should sizzle as soon as it hits the fat. Return to the oven and bake for 15–20 minutes until well-risen and deep golden brown – do not open the oven during cooking.

Carve the meat into chunky slices (3 per person) and serve with the Yorkshire puddings and the juices from the meat. Serve with vegetables such as Vichy carrots and spring onion and horseradish mash.

This glorious recipe can be made as a large pie, or as individual pies for a special occasion. It can be completely made ahead of time – even frozen. Make the stew in advance, top with pastry and refrigerate until ready to put in the oven – the individual pies can be cooking while you eat your starter. If you don't want to use pastry, serve as a stew with plenty of mashed potatoes. Dried wild mushrooms are available in most supermarkets.

steak and wild mushroom pies

50 g dried wild mushrooms

6 tablespoons olive oil or dripping

1 onion, finely chopped

3 garlic cloves, chopped

1 large carrot, finely chopped

2 celery stalks, finely chopped

125 g cubed pancetta or streaky bacon

8 juniper berries, crushed

3 bay leaves

2 tablespoons chopped fresh thyme

2 tablespoons plain white flour

1 kg stewing beef, trimmed
and cut into large cubes

300 ml red wine

2 tablespoons rowan or redcurrant jelly

600 g ready-rolled puff pastry

1 egg, beaten

sea salt and freshly ground black pepper

6 individual pie dishes or 1 large pie dish

2 baking sheets

Serves 6

Put the dried mushrooms in a bowl, just cover with hot water and let soak for 30 minutes. Meanwhile, heat half the oil in a large casserole, add the onion, garlic, carrot and celery and cook for 5–10 minutes until softening. Stir in the pancetta and fry with the vegetables until just beginning to brown. Add the juniper berries, bay leaves and thyme, sprinkle in the flour, mix well and set aside.

Heat the remaining olive oil in a large frying pan and fry the beef quickly (in batches) on all sides until crusty and brown. Transfer to the casserole as you go. When done, deglaze the frying pan with the wine, let bubble, then scrape up the sediment from the bottom of the pan. Pour over the meat and vegetables.

Drain the mushrooms and add to the casserole with 150 ml of the soaking water and the rowan jelly. Season very well with salt and pepper, then stir well. Bring to the boil on top of the stove, then simmer for 1½ hours until tender. Let cool overnight.

Next day, spoon the stew into 6 individual pie dishes. Cut out 6 circles of pastry, a good 3 cm wider than the dishes. Alternatively, use a large pie dish and roll the pastry wider than the dish, as before. Brush the edges of the dishes with beaten egg. Sit the pastry on top of the rim and press over the edge to seal tightly. Brush with more beaten egg, but don't pierce the tops (the steam must be trapped inside). Set the pies on 2 baking sheets and chill for 30 minutes or until ready to bake. Bake at 220°C (425°F) Gas 7 for 20–25 minutes (or 45 minutes to 1 hour for the large pie) until the pastry is risen, crisp and golden brown. Serve hot.

The perfect cook-and-forget roast. The meat is cooked on a bed of rosemary and onions until it is completely tender all the way through – no pink bits – and the onions are melting into the rosemary gravy. Purée the meat juices with the soft onions for a wonderful, creamy sauce.

pot roast leg of lamb
with rosemary and onion gravy

1.5 kg leg of lamb

2 tablespoons olive oil

3 garlic cloves, crushed

2 tablespoons chopped fresh rosemary

3 large rosemary sprigs

2 fresh bay leaves

4 large onions, thinly sliced

300 ml dry white wine

2 teaspoons Dijon mustard

sea salt and freshly ground black pepper

Potatoes Dauphinoise (page 101), to serve

Serves 6

Trim the lamb of any excess fat. Heat the oil in a casserole in which the lamb will fit snugly. Add the lamb and brown it all over. Remove to a plate and let cool.

Crush the garlic and chopped rosemary together with a mortar and pestle. Using a small sharp knife, make little incisions all over the lamb. Push the paste well into these incisions. Season well with salt and pepper.

Put the rosemary sprigs, bay leaves and onions in the casserole and put the lamb on top. Mix the wine with the mustard, then pour into the casserole. Bring to the boil, cover tightly, then cook in a preheated oven at 160°C (325°F) Gas 3 for 1½ hours, turning the lamb over twice.

Raise the oven temperature to 200°C (400°F) Gas 6 and remove the lid from the casserole. Cook for another 30 minutes. The lamb should be very tender and completely cooked through.

Carefully remove the lamb to a serving dish and keep it warm. Skim the fat from the cooking juices and remove the bay leaves and rosemary sprigs. Add a little water if too thick, then bring to the boil, scraping the bottom of the pan to mix in the sediment. Pour the sauce into a blender or food processor and blend until smooth. Taste and season with salt and pepper. Serve with the lamb. Potatoes Dauphinoise make a good partner.

This moist and tender cut of pork is basted throughout cooking with the mahogany-coloured balsamic vinegar and soy cooking juices that give a wonderful colour and flavour to the meat. Roasting first at a high temperature really crisps up the crackling and concentrates the sauce. If you buy the meat from a butcher, ask him for the bones.

roast loin of pork
with balsamic vinegar

1.75 kg loin of pork
1 tablespoon olive oil
300 ml dry white wine
75 ml balsamic vinegar
75 ml soy sauce
sea salt and freshly ground black pepper

Serves 6

Ask the butcher to remove the rind and score it for crackling, then bone the loin and tie up the meat, but to give you the bones. Weigh the meat and calculate the cooking time, allowing 25 minutes to every 500 g.

Heat the oil in a frying pan, add the meat, brown it all over, then transfer to a roasting pan and pour the wine, vinegar and soy sauce over the pork.

Put the bones in another roasting pan, convex side up. Rub the pork rind with salt, then drape it over the pork bones. Put the pan of crackling on the top shelf of the oven, and the meat on the bottom to middle shelf. Roast in a preheated oven at 220°C (425°F) Gas 7 for 30 minutes, baste the pork, then reduce the heat to 190°C (375°F) Gas 5, and roast for the remaining calculated time, basting the pork loin every 20 minutes. When cooked, serve the pork thickly sliced with shards of crunchy crackling and dark pan juices seasoned with freshly ground black pepper.

Reduced balsamic vinegar To make cheap balsamic vinegar taste rich and delicious, turn it into a concentrated syrup by pouring the whole bottle into a saucepan. Open the kitchen window or turn on the extractor fan, then boil hard until reduced by half and looking syrupy. Let cool, then pour into a jar and store in the refrigerator. This is wonderful added to stews, soups and dressings.

vegetarian

This can all be assembled the day before, refrigerated and put in the oven at the last moment. You can vary the type of cheese, as long as it is a soft one.

ricotta, basil and cherry tomato cannelloni

750 g ripe cherry tomatoes, whole, plus 350 g vine-ripened tomatoes, thinly sliced (you need 24 slices)

5 tablespoons good olive oil

2 teaspoons dried oregano

2 teaspoons sugar

300 g ricotta cheese

6 tablespoons fresh red or green pesto (page 135)

12 sheets of fresh lasagne

3 tablespoons freshly grated Parmesan cheese

a handful of basil leaves

sea salt and freshly ground black pepper

green salad, to serve

a baking dish, 20 x 25 cm, lightly oiled

Serves 4

Cut 250 g of the whole cherry tomatoes in half and set aside for the top.

Heat the oil in a frying pan, add the uncut tomatoes (they will splutter a little) and cover tightly. Cook over high heat, shaking the pan occasionally, for 5 minutes until the tomatoes start to break down. Uncover and stir in the oregano, sugar, salt and pepper. Set aside.

Soften the cheese in a bowl and beat in the pesto. Put all the sheets of lasagne on a work surface and spread the cheese mixture evenly over them. Put 2 tomato slices on each sheet, season well and roll up from the narrow side like a Swiss roll. Spoon half the tomato sauce in the bottom of the baking dish. Put the pasta rolls on top of the sauce, then spoon over the remaining sauce. Dot with the reserved cherry tomato halves and cover with foil.

Bake in a preheated oven at 220°C (425°F) Gas 7 for 25–30 minutes. Uncover, sprinkle with the Parmesan and bake or grill for a further 10 minutes until beginning to brown. Remove from the oven and let stand for 10 minutes before serving.

Top with the basil and serve with a crisp green salad.

Note If using dried lasagne sheets, cook in boiling salted water according to the packet instructions. Carefully lift them out of the water and drain through a colander. Transfer to a bowl of cold water. Lift out and drain each sheet before spreading with the cheese mixture.

The bigger and darker the mushrooms, the better their flavour. Laced with garlic and a hint of rosemary, they are sublime. Creamy fresh goats' cheese cuts the richness of the filling. I used walnuts, but any nuts will do.

mushroom, walnut and goats' cheese tart

1 recipe Shortcrust Pastry (see note)

75 g unsalted butter

1 onion, thinly sliced

2 garlic cloves, finely chopped

1 tablespoon chopped fresh rosemary

500 g large, dark portobello mushrooms, sliced

finely grated zest and juice of 1 unwaxed lemon

3 large eggs, beaten

250 g mild goats' cheese, softened

100 g walnuts, coarsely chopped

sea salt and freshly ground black pepper

tomato and rocket salad, to serve

a deep fluted tart tin, 25 cm diameter

baking parchment and baking beans

Serves 6

Put the pastry on a floured work surface and roll it out thinly. Use to line the tart tin. Prick the base, then cover with baking parchment and baking beans. Bake in a preheated oven at 200°C (400°F) Gas 6 for 10–12 minutes, then remove from the oven, remove the paper and beans and return to the oven to cook for another 5–7 minutes. The tart shell can be made in advance.

When ready to cook the tart, keep the oven heat at 200°C (400°F) Gas 6. Melt the butter in a frying pan, add the onion, then the garlic and fry for 10 minutes until soft and golden. Stir in the rosemary. Add the mushrooms, lemon zest and juice, salt and pepper and fry over medium heat for 5 minutes until the mushrooms are tender and the liquid has evaporated. Let cool slightly.

Put the eggs and half the goats' cheese in a bowl, beat well, then stir into the mushroom mixture. Season well. Pour into the baked pastry case and spread evenly. Slice the remaining goats' cheese thinly and dot all over the surface. Sprinkle with the chopped walnuts and bake in the preheated oven for 20–25 minutes until set and golden on top. Serve warm with tomato and rocket salad.

Note Shortcrust Pastry
Sift 250 g plain flour and a pinch of salt into a food processor. Rub in 125 g unsalted butter (chilled and chopped) until the mixture looks like breadcrumbs (or process for 30 seconds). Add 2–3 tablespoons chilled water and mix lightly with a knife to bring the pastry together (or process for 10 seconds). If necessary, add another tablespoon of water and repeat. Knead lightly on a floured work surface, then shape into a flattened ball, wrap in clingfilm and chill for at least 30 minutes before rolling out.

Good felafel are light and full of flavour. It really is worthwhile using dried and soaked chickpeas – canned ones will make the mix too soft and claggy. The felafel should be bright green with herbs, and are a wonderful snack to serve with drinks, as well as making an ideal protein-rich main course or a light lunch for vegetarians.

felafel with avocado, tomato and red onion salsa

250 g dried chickpeas, soaked in cold water for 24 hours

2 garlic cloves, crushed

1 teaspoon ground cumin

½ teaspoon ground coriander

a pinch of chilli powder (optional)

½ teaspoon bicarbonate of soda

2 spring onions, very finely chopped

3 tablespoons chopped fresh flat leaf parsley

3 tablespoons chopped fresh coriander

sea salt and freshly ground black pepper

sunflower oil for deep-frying

pita bread, to serve

Avocado, tomato and red onion salsa

4 ripe tomatoes

1 large ripe avocado

½ red onion, finely chopped

½ small fresh red chilli, halved, deseeded and very finely chopped

3 tablespoons chopped fresh coriander

finely grated zest and juice of 1 unwaxed lime

2–3 tablespoons olive oil

sea salt and freshly ground black pepper

a tray lined with clingfilm

an electric deep-fryer (optional)

Serves 4

Start the day before. Soak the chickpeas in plenty of cold water. The next day, drain them very well and roll in kitchen paper to dry them. Transfer to a food processor, add the garlic, cumin, coriander, chilli powder and bicarbonate of soda and blend to a smooth paste. Taste and season well with salt and pepper. Tip into a bowl, cover and let rest for 30 minutes.

Add the spring onions, parsley and coriander to the chickpea paste, beat well, then knead the mixture to bring it together. Scoop out small lumps and make into flat, round cakes – as small or large as you like – and put them on the lined tray. Cover and chill for 15 minutes.

Meanwhile, to make the salsa, cut the tomatoes in half, deseed them, then chop finely and put in a bowl. Chop the avocado and add to the bowl. Add the onion, chilli and coriander and stir gently. Put the lime juice, zest, olive oil, salt and pepper in a small bowl and mix well. Pour over the tomato mixture, fold gently and set aside.

Fill a saucepan or deep-fryer one-third full with the oil, or to the manufacturer's recommended level. Heat to 180°C (355°F) or until a cube of bread browns in 30 seconds. Cook, in batches if necessary, for 2–3 minutes until they are crisp and brown, turning them over once. Lift out with a slotted spoon and drain on kitchen paper. Serve hot or warm, with pita bread and the salsa.

You couldn't find a simpler pasta dish to prepare. It makes a very elegant starter when served in small portions, or a filling main course. Try to keep the butter melted for as long as possible so the lemon oil is fully infused.

tagliolini with lemon and green olives

2 unwaxed lemons

125 g unsalted butter

125 g green olives, chopped

1 tablespoon chopped fresh lemon thyme (optional)

250 g pasta such as egg tagliolini, paglia e fieno or linguine

50 g grated Parmesan or pecorino cheese, plus extra to serve

sea salt and freshly ground black pepper

Serves 4 as a starter; 2 as a main course

Grate the zest from the lemons, making sure you grate only the yellow zest and not the bitter white pith.

Melt the butter slowly in a stainless steel or non-reactive pan and add the grated zest. Leave over a very gentle heat or in a warm place to infuse for at least 2 hours (or for as long as you have), re-melting if necessary.

When ready to eat, strain the melted butter (reheating if necessary), then add the chopped olives, lemon thyme, if using, and salt and pepper to taste. Keep it warm.

Cook the pasta in a large saucepan of boiling salted water, according to the packet instructions. Drain, reserving 2–3 tablespoons of the cooking water. Toss the pasta with the lemon and olive butter, cheese, more pepper if you like, and some of the reserved cooking water if it looks too dry. Serve immediately with extra cheese.

Variations
• Add lots of cracked black pepper to the strained lemon butter. Omit the olives and add 75 g chopped rocket leaves and plenty of grated Parmesan.
• Instead of the lemon zest, infuse bay leaves in the butter and add 250 g halved cherry tomatoes.

3 tablespoons olive oil

1.5 kg mild onions, finely sliced

3 garlic cloves, chopped

1 teaspoon dried herbes de Provence

Tomato sauce

2 tablespoons olive oil

800g canned chopped tomatoes

3 tablespoons tomato purée

1 tablespoon capers, rinsed and drained

1 teaspoon Harissa Sauce (page136) (optional)

150 ml dry white wine

sea salt and freshly ground black pepper

Yeast dough

7g fresh yeast, 1 teaspoon fast-action
(easy-blend) dried yeast
or 2 teaspoons ordinary dried yeast

a pinch of sugar

150 g plain flour, plus extra for rolling

50 g unsalted butter, chilled and chopped

1 medium egg, beaten

a pinch of sea salt

To finish

red pepper strips or
about 10 anchovy fillets (optional)

extra olive oil, for drizzling

12–18 small black olives

a Swiss roll tin, 33 x 20 cm

Serves 4–6

This is my favourite summer picnic food – the taste of the seaside in the South of France. Soft, sweet onions scented with Provençal herbs are spread over a layer of concentrated sunshine (tomato sauce), then topped with red pepper strips or sea-salty anchovies and black olives, all on a thin yeasty base. Cut into squares and wrap in foil to take on a picnic.

pissaladière

Heat the oil in a large saucepan, add the onions and garlic and stir well to coat with the oil. Add 1–2 tablespoons water, cover tightly and simmer over very low heat for about 1 hour until meltingly soft. Stir them from time to time to prevent them sticking, but don't let them colour. Add a little more water if they look dry. Stir in the herbs. Drain the mixture into a sieve over a bowl and reserve the liquid for the yeast dough.

To make the tomato sauce, heat the oil in a saucepan, add the olive oil, tomatoes, tomato purée, capers, harissa sauce, if using, white wine, salt and pepper. Mix well and bring to the boil. Simmer, uncovered, for about 1 hour, stirring occasionally, until well reduced and very thick. Taste and adjust the seasoning. Set aside.

To make the yeast dough, cream the fresh yeast in a bowl with the sugar, then whisk in 3 tablespoons of the warmed reserved onion liquid. Leave for 10 minutes until frothy. For other yeasts, use according to the packet instructions. Sift the flour into a bowl and rub in the butter. Make a hollow in the centre, add the egg, yeast mixture and a pinch of salt, and mix to a very soft dough – add more onion liquid if it seems dry. Knead in the bowl for 1–2 minutes until smooth. Put in an oiled bowl, cover with clingfilm and let rise for 1 hour or until doubled in size.

Knock back the dough, knead lightly, then roll out on a lightly floured surface. Use to line the tin, pushing the dough well up the edges. Spread the reduced tomato sauce thinly over the dough base. Cover with the onions. Arrange the red pepper strips, if using, in a lattice on top of the onions. Alternatively, cut the anchovy fillets in half lengthways and use them instead. Drizzle with a little olive oil and bake in a preheated oven at 190°C (375°F) Gas 5 for about 1 hour until the pastry is golden and crisp. Arrange the olives on top and serve warm or cold.

Not only is this completely vegetarian, but carnivores love it too. It is delicious, rich and substantial enough to serve on a cold winter's night. Sometimes, I cook some thinly sliced onions to a crisp caramel and scatter these on top. Mint tea (page 132) is delicious to drink after this dish.

sesame and mint couscous
with winter vegetables

25 g unsalted butter

2 garlic cloves, finely crushed

1 tablespoon sweet paprika

2 teaspoons cumin

½ teaspoon ground ginger

1 teaspoon sea salt

1 teaspoon freshly ground black pepper

2 bay leaves

2 tablespoons tomato purée

400 g canned chopped tomatoes

2 whole fresh green chillies

2 thick carrots, peeled, quartered and cut into finger lengths

2 thick parsnips, peeled, quartered and cut into finger lengths

500 g potatoes, peeled and cut into 5 cm chunks

2 thick courgettes, quartered and cut into finger lengths

200 g butternut or pumpkin, peeled, deseeded and cut into 5 cm chunks

2 tablespoons harissa sauce mixed with 125 ml hot water, to serve

Sesame and mint couscous

375 g instant couscous

500 ml boiling water

125 g butter, cubed

4 tablespoons chopped fresh mint

3 tablespoons toasted sesame seeds

sea salt and freshly ground black pepper

Serves 6

Melt the butter in a heavy casserole, add the garlic and cook for 1 minute over medium heat. Add the paprika, cumin, ginger, salt, pepper, bay leaves, tomato purée and canned tomatoes and stir well. Bring to the boil and add the chillies, carrots and parsnips.

Pour in enough water to cover (about 400 ml), bring to the boil, part-cover with a lid, then simmer gently for 20 minutes. Add the potatoes, courgettes and butternut, pushing them under the liquid, and cook for a further 20 minutes or until the potatoes are tender. Do not overcook or the vegetables will disintegrate.

Meanwhile, put the couscous in a bowl. Pour the boiling water into a measuring jug, stir in the butter and mint, then pour evenly over the couscous. Cover tightly with clingfilm and let stand for 5 minutes.

Uncover the couscous and fluff up the grains with a fork. Stir in the sesame seeds, taste and season well with salt and pepper. Pile the couscous onto a large serving platter, make a hollow in the centre and heap the spicy vegetable stew into the middle. Serve immediately with the harissa sauce mixture in a small bowl.

Note Harissa sauce is widely available in larger supermarkets, delis and Middle Eastern stores. To make your own, see the recipe on page 136.

This pretty gratin is bursting with all the flavours of the sun and is based on the tian, a Provençal classic. You can vary the vegetables according to whatever you have available. It's good with courgettes, peppers, potatoes or onions – and there are even non-vegetarian versions that include boneless chicken pieces. This makes a wonderful dish to serve on its own with a green salad and plenty of focaccia.

tomato and aubergine gratin
with tomato and chilli pesto

2 medium aubergines

500 g ripe red tomatoes

about 150 ml olive oil

1 recipe Tomato and Chilli Pesto (page 135)

4 tablespoons chopped fresh basil

125 g freshly grated Parmesan cheese

sea salt and freshly ground black pepper

a shallow ovenproof dish, buttered

Serves 4

Using a sharp knife, cut the aubergine into 5 mm slices. Sprinkle with salt and put in a colander to drain for 30 minutes. Rinse well and pat dry with kitchen paper.

Brush the aubergines with olive oil and grill on both sides until brown. Drain on kitchen paper.

Cut the tomatoes in half through the middle.

Arrange a layer of aubergines in the dish, followed by a few spoonfuls of pesto, then a layer of tomatoes and the basil. Sprinkle with Parmesan. Season with salt and pepper, then repeat, finishing with a layer of aubergines. Sprinkle with the remaining Parmesan.

Bake in a preheated oven at 200°C (400°F) Gas 6 for 25–30 minutes until browned and bubbling on top. Cool slightly, then serve warm, or let cool completely and serve chilled as a salad.

vegetables and salads

This Caesar isn't Roman – it was invented in 1924 by restaurateur Caesar Cardini, 'south of the border, down Mexico way'. In fact, the only thing Roman about it is the kind of lettuce used – cos or romaine lettuce.

caesar salad

1 cos lettuce

150 ml olive oil

2 large garlic cloves, crushed

2 tablespoons freshly squeezed lemon juice, from about ½ large lemon

½ teaspoon Dijon mustard

2 anchovy fillets in oil, drained

1 large egg yolk

2 slices of stale bread, crusts removed, cubed

2 tablespoon freshly grated Parmesan cheese

sea salt and freshly ground black pepper

Serves 4

Pull the leaves off the lettuce, wash and tear into bite-sized pieces. Spin in a salad spinner or dry on kitchen paper. Store in a sealed plastic bag in the refrigerator to keep it crisp.

Put 3 tablespoons olive oil in a blender or food processor and add half the garlic, the lemon juice, mustard, anchovies and egg yolk. Blend until smooth, then transfer to a jug, taste and season with salt and pepper.

Pour the remaining olive oil into a frying pan, add the remaining garlic and heat until it starts to sizzle. Scoop out the garlic, then add the cubed bread. Fry until golden, keeping the pieces on the move while they are cooking. Lift out and drain on kitchen paper.

Stir the dressing, pour over the salad leaves, toss well, then transfer to a bowl. Add the croutons and sprinkle with the Parmesan. Serve immediately.

If anchovies don't appeal, liven up the dressing with a dash of Worcestershire sauce. You can use other kinds of salad leaves, such as radicchio, iceberg or Chinese leaves – just remember that they must be crisp to bring out the crunchiness of the salad.

Always make dressings fresh Whisk the ingredients in the bottom of the salad bowl, then add the leaves and toss well to coat.

This is a great prepare-ahead dish for a crowd. You can use any type of Oriental noodle for this; there are so many available today – some dried, some ready-to-use. Even Italian pasta works well with this peanut sauce.

cold noodles
with peanut sauce

500 g noodles

1 tablespoon sesame oil or sunflower oil

1 teaspoon Szechuan peppercorns

3 cm fresh ginger, peeled and coarsely chopped

2 large juicy garlic cloves

4 tablespoons smooth peanut butter

4 tablespoons soy sauce

3 teaspoons chilli oil (chilli-flavoured oil)

½ teaspoon sea salt

2 teaspoons sugar

6 spring onions, finely sliced diagonally

3 tablespoons raw peanuts, toasted and coarsely chopped

Serves 4

Cook the noodles according to the packet instructions, depending on type. Drain, rinse well and let drain for a couple of minutes. Add a little sesame oil and toss gently.

Heat a small frying pan and toast the Szechuan peppercorns for a couple of minutes until they smell aromatic and begin to smoke a little. Do not let them burn. Tip into a bowl and let cool. Grind to a powder using a pepper grinder or mortar and pestle.

Transfer to a food processor, add the ginger, garlic, peanut butter, soy sauce, chilli oil, salt, sugar and 140 ml warm water and blend until smooth and creamy. Beat in extra warm water if too thick. Add the sauce to the noodles, toss well, then transfer to a serving dish and sprinkle the spring onions and peanuts on top.

> **Szechuan peppercorns**, sometimes known as Chinese pepper or fagara, are little brown berries that are dried and roasted to bring out their spicy, woody flavour. They are readily available in larger supermarkets. If you can't find them, use black pepper and a tiny pinch of Chinese five-spice powder.

ratatouille

One of those reliable recipes that just gets better as it matures, ratatouille can be served with many dishes, and also by itself with lots of crusty bread. Don't use green peppers – they are too bitter.

2 aubergines

3 peppers (red, yellow or orange)

3 tablespoons olive oil

2 large onions, thinly sliced

2 garlic cloves, crushed

2 teaspoons finely crushed coriander seeds

5 tablespoons white wine

400 g canned chopped tomatoes

1 teaspoon sugar

about 20 Greek-style dry-cured black olives

sea salt and freshly ground black pepper

parsley leaves, to serve (optional)

Serves 6

Cut the aubergines into large, bite-sized pieces, put them in a colander, sprinkle well with salt and let drain for 1 hour. Cut the peppers in half, remove the white membrane and seeds and slice the flesh into thick strips.

Heat the olive oil in a heatproof casserole and fry the onions, crushed garlic and coriander seeds until soft and transparent, but not coloured. Add the wine and boil to reduce.

Meanwhile, rinse and drain the aubergines and dry on kitchen paper. Add the peppers and aubergines to the casserole and cook for about 10 minutes, stirring occasionally until softening around the edges, but not browning. Add the tomatoes, sugar and olives. Heat to simmering point, season well with salt and pepper, then half-cover and cook for about 25 minutes. Add the parsley, if using, and serve hot or cold.

potatoes dauphinoise

This reheats well, so make it in advance to be sure it is perfectly cooked. A time-saving trick is to cover the dish and microwave on HIGH for 10 minutes, then finish it off in the oven for 45 minutes.

50 g unsalted butter, for greasing the dish

1 kg waxy potatoes (Desirée are good), peeled and thinly sliced

125 g freshly grated Parmesan cheese

freshly grated nutmeg

300 ml double cream

sea salt and freshly ground black pepper

a shallow ovenproof dish, well buttered

Serves 6

Layer the potatoes in the dish, seasoning each layer with cheese, nutmeg, salt and pepper. Pour over the cream and sprinkle any remaining cheese over the top. If the dish will stand it, set it on top of the stove and lightly warm through before baking in a preheated oven at 160°C (325°F) Gas 3 for about 1 hour or until the potatoes are tender and the top is golden and crisp.

green rice

Basmati rice is one of the most flavourful varieties there are, especially when cooked properly. Follow this recipe and you will never have soggy rice again. Green herbs and spinach add an extra dimension.

300 g basmati rice
4 tablespoons coarsely chopped green herbs, such as parsley and coriander
100 g frozen chopped spinach, thawed
1 tablespoon sunflower oil

Serves 4

Bring a huge saucepan of cold salted water to the boil. The size of the pan is crucial – the larger the pan, the more water it holds, therefore the rice moves around as it cooks and doesn't stick. Wash the rice under cold running water until the water runs clear. Drain. Add the rice to the boiling water, return to a rolling boil and stir once. Boil for exactly 8 minutes then drain well, return to the pan, stir in the herbs, spinach and oil, then quickly put on a tight-fitting lid. Let steam in its own heat for another 10 minutes, then lightly fluff up with a fork. Serve immediately.

perfect mashed potatoes

The secret of perfect mash is the right potato – a floury variety that fluffs up properly. Older potatoes work better than new and make sure that they are thoroughly cooked or the mash will be lumpy. The mash will keep warm in a very cool oven – 120°C (250°F) Gas ½ – for up to 2 hours if covered with buttered foil. Otherwise, cool and reheat gently, beating in extra melted butter and hot milk. If adding herbs, beat in just before serving.

750 g floury potatoes, quartered
55 g unsalted butter
75–100 ml milk
sea salt and freshly ground black pepper

Serves 4

Preheat the oven to 150°C (300°F) Gas Mark 2. Put the potatoes in a saucepan of salted cold water and bring to the boil. As soon as the water comes to the boil, reduce to a simmer (it's important not to cook the potatoes too quickly) and cook for about 20 minutes. When perfectly done, the point of a sharp knife should glide into the centre.

Drain in a colander, then set over the hot pan to steam and dry out. Tip the potatoes back into the hot pan and crush with a potato masher or pass them through a mouli or ricer into the pan. Melt the butter in the milk. Using a wooden spoon, beat the butter and milk into the mash – an electric hand-mixer sometimes helps here. Season, pile into a warm dish and serve immediately.

Variation Spring Onion and Horseradish Mash
Beat in 3 tablespoons chopped spring onions sautéed in butter and 2 tablespoons creamed horseradish.

vichy carrots
with fresh ginger

These buttery carrots almost caramelize as they cook, so the ginger adds a spicy punch to cut through the rich sweetness.

1 kg carrots

2 tablespoons finely chopped fresh ginger

55 g unsalted butter

½ teaspoon sea salt

2 teaspoons caster sugar

freshly ground black pepper

3 tablespoons chopped fresh coriander or parsley

Serves 8

Cut the carrots into batons or thick rounds and put in a saucepan with the ginger, butter, salt and sugar. Half-cover with water, bring to the boil and boil steadily, stirring once or twice, until the water has almost disappeared and the carrots are tender.

Reduce the heat and let the carrots brown a little and caramelize. Season with black pepper and stir in the coriander or parsley. Serve immediately.

Use big old carrots for Vichy, because they will stand up to longer cooking. If using young carrots, keep them whole and leave some of the green tops on for colour.

petits pois à la française

Equally good when made with fresh or frozen peas, this recipe is great for large numbers. The lettuce adds sweetness to the peas. Perfect with fish or lamb – especially in the spring.

250 g green peas, fresh or frozen

1 large Spanish onion, thinly sliced

1 small lettuce, shredded

55 g unsalted butter

1 teaspoon caster sugar

2 tablespoons chopped fresh mint

2 tablespoons chopped fresh parsley

sea salt and freshly ground black pepper

Serves 4

Mix the peas, onion and lettuce together in a casserole. Add 150 ml water, the butter, sugar, salt and pepper. Cover tightly and simmer for 30 minutes or bake in the oven at 160°C (325°F) Gas 3 for 1½ hours until very soft. Stir in the herbs, add salt and pepper to taste, then serve.

barbecued sweetcorn
with chilli lime butter

Messy and meltingly delicious, grilled sweetcorn will be a favourite with a crowd of hungry youngsters. Serve with lots of paper napkins – this is definitely a hands-on dish.

12 ears of corn-on-the-cob, husked

125 g unsalted butter, melted

a large pinch of chilli powder

sea salt and freshly ground black pepper

Chilli lime butter

1 teaspoon sweet chilli sauce

finely grated zest and juice of 2 unwaxed limes

125 g unsalted butter, softened

greaseproof paper

Serves 6

To make the chilli lime butter, put the chilli, lime zest and butter in a bowl and beat well. Season with salt and pepper, then roll into a cylinder between sheets of damp greaseproof paper. Twist the ends and chill for at least 1 hour until hard.

To barbecue the corn, melt the butter in a small saucepan and whisk in the chilli and lime juice. This will be the basting sauce for the corn.

Preheat a barbecue or grill, add the corn and cook for at least 10 minutes, basting and turning until golden brown all over, soft and lightly charred. Slice the chilled butter into disks and serve with the hot grilled corn.

roasted mediterranean vegetables

3 small courgettes

1 medium red pepper, quartered and deseeded

1 medium yellow pepper, quartered and deseeded

2 medium red onions, cut into 8 wedges through the root (keep the roots intact)

1 small aubergine, cut into large cubes

150 ml good olive oil

a few drops balsamic vinegar

2 sprigs of thyme

fresh basil leaves, torn

Serves 4

Cut the courgettes into halves or quarters. Put the peppers, onions and aubergine in a large roasting tin. Pour the oil over the vegetables, add a few drops of balsamic vinegar and toss well. Roast in a preheated oven at 200°C (400°F) Gas 6 for about 35–40 minutes, carefully turning twice, adding the thyme 10 minutes before the vegetables are cooked.

The vegetables should begin to take on colour and be tender but not disintegrating. Season them well with salt and pepper and transfer to a serving dish. Add the torn basil and serve.

sweet things

This has always been one of my favourite cook-in-advance sweet things. Everybody loves it – adults and children alike. Raspberries are delicious with hazelnut and chocolate, but cherries and strawberries would also work well. Keep the cooled meringue in an airtight box until ready to use. You can make this up to one day ahead.

hazelnut and raspberry pavlova
with hot chocolate sauce

4 large egg whites

a pinch of sea salt

225 g caster sugar, plus a little extra, to taste

1 teaspoon cornflour

1 teaspoon vanilla essence

1 teaspoon wine vinegar

100 g toasted chopped hazelnuts, plus extra for sprinkling

250 g raspberries, fresh or frozen and thawed

Chocolate sauce and whipped cream

200 g dark chocolate

650 ml double cream

50 g caster sugar, plus 1 tablespoon extra

30 g unsalted butter

a baking sheet, lined with non-stick baking parchment

Serves 6

Mark the lined baking sheet with a 25 cm circle.

Put the egg whites and salt in a bowl and whisk until very stiff. Gradually whisk in the caster sugar, one large spoonful at a time, making sure the meringue is really 'bouncily' stiff before adding the next spoonful.

Whisk cornflour, vanilla and vinegar into the meringue. Fold in the nuts.

Spoon the meringue into the circle right to the edges, making it as rough as you like, but not too shallow. Make a slight dip in the centre.

Bake in a preheated oven at 140°C (275°F) Gas 1 for about 45 minutes until just beginning to turn the palest brown. Turn off the oven and let cool slowly.

To make the hot chocolate sauce, put the chocolate, 200 ml of the cream, the sugar and butter in a saucepan. Stir until melted. Pour into a jug and keep it warm. Put the 1 tablespoon sugar and remaining 450 ml cream in a bowl and whip until soft peaks form.

Carefully peel the baking parchment from the pavlova and set it on a serving dish. Dollop the cream generously on top and sprinkle with the raspberries. Trail the hot chocolate sauce over the top or serve it separately. Serve immediately.

A gloriously moreish tart with the fruit nestling in a cooked almond filling. This one is made with cherries, but other fruits are also delicious – try fresh apricots or plums, halved and stoned, sliced apples, peaches, pears or no-need-to-soak prunes. Serve with custard, cream or ice cream.

fruit frangipane tart

1 recipe Rich Shortcrust Pastry (see note)

Frangipane

200 g butter, softened

200 g caster sugar

2 large eggs, plus 2 large egg yolks

4 teaspoons kirsch

200 g ground almonds,

4 tablespoons plain flour

450 g fresh cherries

150 ml warm sieved apricot jam

a tart tin, 30 cm diameter

Serves 6–8

Preheat the oven to 200°C (400°F) Gas 6. Preheat a baking sheet. Roll out the pastry and use to line a 30 cm tart tin. Prick the base lightly all over with a fork. Freeze until firm.

To make the frangipane, put the butter and sugar in a food processor and beat until light and fluffy. With the machine running, gradually add the whole eggs, egg yolks and kirsch. Beat in the ground almonds and flour. Spoon the frangipane into the chilled pastry case, spreading it out evenly. Dot with the chosen fruit, pressing down gently until they touch the base. Put on the hot baking sheet for 10–15 minutes until the pastry edges begin to brown. Turn the heat down to 180°C (350°F) Gas 4 and bake for a further 30–35 minutes, until the frangipane is golden brown and set. Transfer to a wire rack to cool. Just before serving, brush the surface with the apricot jam and serve at room temperature.

Note Rich Shortcrust Pastry

Sift 250 g plain flour and ½ teaspoon salt together into a bowl, then rub in 125 g chilled, chopped, unsalted butter. Mix 2 medium egg yolks with 2 tablespoons iced water. Add to the flour, mixing together lightly with a knife. (The pastry must have some water in it or it will be too difficult to handle. If it is still too dry, add a little more water, sprinkling it over the flour mixture 1 tablespoon at a time.)

Turn out the mixture onto a lightly floured work surface. Knead lightly with your hands until smooth, then form into a rough ball. Flatten slightly, then wrap in clingfilm and chill for at least 30 minutes before rolling out. You can also freeze it, then thaw before rolling out. This recipe makes about 400 g pastry, enough to line a tart tin 25–30 cm diameter.

Variation For a Sweet Shortcrust Pastry, sift 2 tablespoons icing sugar with the flour and salt.

mixed nut treacle tart

Incredibly rich, this tart can be packed with whatever kinds of nuts you have available. Serve it as a pudding, as here – or in small slices with coffee.

½ recipe Rich Shortcrust pastry (page 112, note)

5 tablespoons treacle

5 tablespoons maple syrup

finely grated rind and juice of 1 unwaxed orange

100 g ground almonds

150 g mixed whole nuts such as walnuts, hazelnuts, pecans, pine nuts and almonds

a thick baking sheet

a tart tin, 20 cm diameter

Serve 6

Preheat the oven to 190°C (375°F) Gas 5 and put in the baking sheet to heat up.

Roll out the pastry to 5 mm thick. Use to line the tart tin, trim and prick the base. I like to chill the pastry or freeze it at this stage. Put the treacle, maple syrup, orange juice and zest in a saucepan and heat until just warm and runny. Stir in the almonds.

Spread into the frozen pastry case and sprinkle the nuts all over the surface. Transfer to the hot baking sheet in the preheated oven and bake for about 30 minutes or until the filling is just set and the pastry browning at the edges.

Remove from the oven and let cool slightly before serving warm with real custard, clotted cream or crème fraîche.

lemon curd tartlets
with blueberry compote

For a super-easy treat to serve with tea or coffee, or as a simple pudding, keep a stack of ready-made tart shells in an airtight tin, your own lemon curd (so easy to make) in a jar in the refrigerator, plus a pot of blueberry compote (also wonderful to keep as a breakfast standby).

1 recipe Shortcrust Pastry (page 83, note)

1 recipe Lemon Curd (page 141)

Blueberry compote

200 g fresh blueberries

100 g caster sugar

7.5 cm fluted biscuit cutter

12-hole bun tin or muffin tin

Make 12 tartlets

Roll out the pastry thinly and cut out 12 rounds with the fluted biscuit cutter. Use to line a 12-hole bun tin with the pastry, pressing the rounds into the tins: Prick the bases and chill or freeze for 15 minutes. Bake blind without lining with beans, in a preheated oven at 180°C (350°F) Gas 4 for 5–8 minutes. Remove from the oven and let cool.

To make the compote, put the blueberries in a saucepan with 1 tablespoon water and the sugar. Cook over gentle heat until the sugar dissolves, then bring to the boil and boil for 1 minute. Pour into a bowl to cool, then store in a jar in the refrigerator.

When ready to serve, fill the tartlet cases with a dollop of lemon curd, then spoon blueberry compote on top. Eat immediately.

These little creams have a texture like satin, and a rich coffee flavour. They are so easy to make and turn out very easily. Because they contain rich, creamy mascarpone cheese, they are a little firmer than usual.

coffee panna cotta

150 g mascarpone cheese

500 ml double cream

3 tablespoons ground espresso coffee

125 g caster sugar

1 vanilla pod, split

4 tablespoons milk

2 teaspoons powdered gelatine

caramelized walnut halves, to decorate

6 small moulds, 100 ml each, lightly oiled

a baking sheet

Serves 6

Put the mascarpone, cream, espresso coffee, sugar and vanilla pod in a saucepan. Put over low heat until almost but not quite boiling, stirring occasionally. Remove from the heat and leave to infuse for 20 minutes.

Put the milk in another saucepan and add the gelatine. Put over very low heat until the gelatine has dissolved. Stir the dissolved gelatine into the hot cream and mascarpone mixture and strain into a jug.

Pour this hot cream into the lightly oiled moulds, let cool, then refrigerate for several hours or overnight until set.

To serve, carefully loosen the creams and invert onto individual plates. Decorate with the walnut halves, then serve at once.

> **To caramelize walnut halves**, melt 100 g caster sugar with 3 tablespoons water until completely dissolved. Bring to the boil, then boil rapidly until the sugar starts to smoke and turn a golden caramel colour. Quickly stir in 6 walnut halves to coat. Lift each half out with a fork and leave to harden on non-stick baking parchment.

There's so much exotic fruit around in the winter, which is lucky for us because temperate climate varieties disappear at that time. In this recipe, brightly coloured fruits are tossed in an unusual fragrant lemongrass and lime syrup, then piled on top of a light yet rich mango mousse. It makes a refreshing end to a big meal or buffet.

mango mousse
with tropical fruit salad

350 g ripe mango flesh or purée

1 tablespoon caster sugar

finely grated zest and juice of 2 unwaxed limes

7 g powdered gelatine (1 tablespoon)

150 ml double cream, lightly whipped

2 egg whites

Lemongrass syrup

125 g sugar

½ stick of lemongrass, bruised with a rolling pin

finely grated zest and juice of 1 unwaxed lime

Tropical fruit salad

1 very ripe red pomegranate

a selection of fresh exotic fruit, such as papaya, pineapple, yellow melon, lychees and grapes (you will need about 75 g prepared fruit per person)

Serves 4

Put the mangoes in a blender or food processor, add the sugar and lime zest and juice and blend to make a smooth, soft purée. Taste and add more sugar if necessary.

Put 3 tablespoons water in a small saucepan, sprinkle with the gelatine and leave for 5 minutes to swell and sponge. Dissolve the gelatine over low heat without boiling until it is liquid and clear, then stir it into the mango purée. Chill for 15 minutes to set slightly, then fold in the lightly whipped cream. Whisk the egg whites until just holding a soft peak and carefully fold into the mango mixture. Spoon into individual glasses, leaving enough room to top with fruit salad. Chill in the refrigerator for 2–3 hours until set.

Meanwhile, to make the lemongrass syrup, put the sugar in a small heavy saucepan, add 300 ml water and melt over low heat. When the sugar has completely dissolved, add the lemongrass, increase the heat and boil for about 2–3 minutes until the syrup feels slippery when tested between the fingers. Remove from the heat, remove the lemongrass and add the lime juice. Let cool, then stir in the lime zest. Chill.

To prepare the pomegranate, cut in half, then remove the red seeds and reserve them. Discard the skin and pith. To prepare the other fruit, peel, deseed, cut into slices or chunks and put in a bowl. Carefully mix all the fruit together and add the chilled syrup. Mix again to coat, then chill in the refrigerator.

To serve, spoon the fruit salad on top of the set mousses and sprinkle with the pomegranate seeds.

brown sugar meringues

Make these ahead, keep in airtight tin, then sandwich together with cream – handy for last-minute puddings.

4 egg whites
125 g caster sugar
125 g light soft brown sugar

a baking sheet lined with non-stick baking parchment

Makes 12

Put the egg whites in a large bowl and whisk until very stiff but not dry. Mix the caster sugar and brown sugar, then gradually whisk in the combined sugars, spoonful by spoonful, letting the mixture become very stiff between each addition.

Spoon 12 large meringues onto the baking parchment. Bake in a preheated oven at 110°C (225°F) Gas Mark ¼ for 3–4 hours until thoroughly dried out.

Remove the meringues from the oven and let cool on the parchment. Carefully lift off when cool and store in an airtight container until required.

baked bananas
with sultana rum ice cream

Adults and kids alike adore baked bananas. This dish takes a Girl Guide campfire recipe to previously unknown heights of sophistication with sultanas soaked in rum until plump and juicy. For children, try soaking the dried fruit in a fruit juice cocktail instead of rum.The sultanas can be soaked well beforehand and kept in a jar in the refrigerator.

200 g sultanas
300 ml dark rum
2 cartons very good quality real-vanilla ice cream, 600 ml each, softened
12 hard butterscotch sweets
6 small perfect bananas

Serve 6

Put the sultanas and rum in a saucepan, bring to the boil, then cover and let cool and swell for 2–3 hours. Mix half of these into the softened ice cream and replace in the freezer. Reserve the remainder, cover and chill until needed.

Put the butterscotch sweets in a plastic bag and crush with a rolling pin. Cut a strip of skin 1 cm wide lengthways down the inside curve of each banana, leaving it attached at the stalk end. Scoop out a little of the banana and sprinkle with the crushed butterscotch sweets. Bake in a preheated oven at 180°C (350°F) Gas 4 for 10–15 minutes. Serve the bananas with a scoop of the ice cream and a spoonful of the rum-soaked sultanas.

chocolate chilli truffles

I like to pass round a mound of these surprisingly warm and mysterious truffles instead of a pudding.

275 g plain dark chocolate
50 g unsalted butter, cubed
300 ml double cream
¼ teaspoon ground hot chilli powder
2 tablespoons chilli vodka
cocoa powder, for coating

a shallow tray and paper cases

Makes about 20

Put the chocolate, butter, cream and chilli in a bowl set over a saucepan of simmering water. Heat until melted – the mixture should be just tepid. Stir occasionally (overmixing will make the mixture grainy). Stir in the vodka.

Pour into a shallow tray and refrigerate until firm. Scoop out teaspoons of mixture, roll into rough balls and chill. Sift the cocoa powder onto a plate. Carefully roll each truffle in the cocoa. Chill until set. Put in paper cases and store in an airtight container in the refrigerator for up to 2 weeks. They may also be frozen for up to 3 months.

Note Candied Bird's Eye Chillies
These are easy to make and are always quite a talking point served with the truffles. Remember, they are very hot! Dissolve 250 g sugar in 300 ml water in medium saucepan. Bring to the boil for 1 minute. Add 50 g whole bird's eye chillies and bring to the boil. Simmer for 15 minutes, then turn off the heat and leave to soak in the syrup for 24 hours. Lift out of the syrup with a fork, drain well and arrange on non-stick baking parchment. Use immediately while still shiny or roll them in a little extra sugar to coat and let dry at room temperature for 24 hours. Store in layers in an airtight box for up to 1 month.

chinese fortune cookies

These are great fun to make for a surprise ending to a dinner party, for someone's birthday or just to start the New Year.

100 g plain flour
¼ teaspoon sea salt
2 tablespoons cornflour
6 tablespoons sugar
2 egg whites
100 ml olive oil
6 lucky messages written on strips of coloured paper

a baking sheet, lightly oiled or lined with non-stick baking parchment

Makes 6

Sift the flour, salt, cornflour and sugar together into a bowl. Whisk the egg white in a second bowl with the olive oil and 3 tablespoons water, then beat into the flour until smooth.

Using a tablespoon of batter for each cookie, and cooking no more than 2 at a time, spread out thinly into 3-inch rounds on the prepared baking sheet.

Bake in a preheated oven at 180°C (350°F) Gas 4 for about 5 minutes or until the edges are just browning. Working quickly, lay a paper message across the centre of each cookie, fold in half over the paper with the help of a palette knife. Hold the rounded edges of semicircle between thumb and forefinger. Put the forefinger of your other hand at the centre of the folded edge and push in, making sure that the solid sides of the cookie puff out. Work quickly because the biscuits become brittle as they cool.

Let the cookies cool completely on a wire rack, then store in an airtight container.

drinks

real old-fashioned lemonade

Make this sensational summer drink when lemons
are ripe and plentiful. Leave the lemons on a warm
windowsill for a few days to sweeten them up and
develop their flavour. You can make this a day or two
ahead – it MUST be served as cold as possible.

3 unwaxed lemons, scrubbed in warm water

200 g sugar

1 litre boiling water

sprigs of mint or lemon balm (optional)

Makes about 1.25 litres

Using a potato peeler, remove the yellow zest from the lemons
in long strips, avoiding any bitter white pith. Put it in a large
heatproof jug, add the sugar and pour over the boiling water.
Stir well to dissolve the sugar, cover and let cool completely.
Squeeze the juice from the lemons, strain and set aside. When
the lemon-scented water is cold, stir in the lemon juice and
strain into a jug. Chill well and serve poured over ice, perhaps
with a sprig of mint or lemon balm.

pear, apple and kiwifruit juice with fresh ginger

This utterly delicious juice combo is one of my
favourite ways to start the day – the ginger adds a
surprising warm and lively note. Kiwifruit contains
large amounts of vitamin C, and I sometimes add
a little watercress or rocket for a green, peppery hit.
Juices and smoothies taste much better if the fruit is
only just ripe (or even a little underripe); if too ripe,
the taste will be dull. Make this recipe in a juicer if
you have one, or make into a yoghurt smoothie in
a blender, in which case it will serve two.

1 not-too-ripe pear

1 apple

2 not-too-ripe kiwifruit

2.5 cm piece of fresh ginger, peeled and
coarsely chopped

Serves 1

Juicer Method Peel and core the pear and apple and cut them
into 6 wedges each. Peel and quarter the kiwifruit. Put the pear
through the juicer first, followed by the ginger, kiwifruit and finally
the apple. Stir well before serving, because it can separate.
Drink as soon a possible and just feel those vitamins coursing
through your body!

Blender Smoothie Put all the prepared fruits and ginger in a
blender with 150 ml plain yoghurt. Blend until smooth, adding
a squeeze of lemon juice or a little salt to taste

pussyfoot

Pussyfoot is one of the best non-alcoholic drinks
I know, and greatly appreciated by designated
drivers and pregnant women. It is grown-up looking
and very refreshing, thanks to the mellowing effect
of the grenadine (sweet pomegranate syrup). Make
sure the juices are freshly squeezed – bottled or
carton juice just will not do. Leave out the egg yolk
if there's any risk involved – it won't matter greatly,
you can always add a tablespoon of cream.

50 ml freshly squeezed orange juice
25 ml freshly squeezed lemon juice
25 ml freshly squeezed lime juice
1–2 tablespoons grenadine
1 free-range egg yolk (optional)
ice cubes

Makes 1

Pour the orange, lemon and lime juices, grenadine and optional
egg yolk into a cocktail shaker half-filled with ice cubes. Shake
well and strain into a glass filled with more ice cubes.

Variation Add a dash of sparkling water or lemonade for bit of
festive fizz.

glögg

This comforting, heart-warming drink is served in cafés in Denmark and Sweden to cheer up bleak winter days. It has a miraculous effect.

2 bottles medium red wine, 750 ml each

125 g sugar

150–200 g mixed raisins and slivered blanched almonds

1 cinnamon stick

4 cloves

8 cardamom pods, lightly crushed

2.5 cm piece of fresh ginger, lightly smashed

200 ml schnapps or vodka

100 ml brandy or cognac

a muslin bag and kitchen string

Serves 8

Pour 1 bottle of red wine into a non-reactive bowl or saucepan. Add the sugar, raisins and almonds and stir to dissolve the sugar. Put the spices in a muslin bag (or clean J-cloth), tie with string and add to the wine. Leave to infuse for a couple of hours if possible.

Heat the wine until almost boiling, then cover and leave to infuse for at least 30 minutes (you can also do this in the morning if serving it at night). When ready, remove the spice bag and pour in the remaining bottle of wine, the schnapps and brandy. Reheat until almost boiling and serve hot in glass cups with spoons to eat the raisins and almonds.

What would we do for a celebration if champagne had never been invented? A real champagne cocktail can be lethal, so don't plan on serving more than two before a meal – trust me.

champagne cocktails

1 sugar cube

Angostura Bitters

1 teaspoon brandy

cold champagne or sparkling wine

Serves 1

Put a sugar cube in the glass. Add a couple of drops of Bitters, then the brandy and top up with cold champagne.

I use tangerine, mandarin or tangelo slices for this sangria, because they add a really exotic touch to the drink, but remember that it's crucial to marinate the base mixture overnight to infuse all the fantastic summery flavours. Make large quantities because people really love it. Sometimes I add Italian limoncello instead of orange liqueur.

white wine sangria

1 bottle dry but full-bodied white wine, 750 ml

2 tablespoons sugar (or to taste)

at least 3 tablespoons orange liqueur

2 small unwaxed oranges, tangerines or tangelos, sliced

2 unwaxed lemons, sliced

250 ml chilled soda water, sparkling water or chilled sparkling wine

To serve

apple and peach slices or wedges

sprigs of mint

Makes 1 litre

Put the wine, sugar, liqueur, oranges and lemons in a large jug. Stir, cover and refrigerate overnight. Strain or not, as you wish, into another jug, then add ice and top up with soda water or chilled sparkling wine. Add apple and peach slices and sprigs of mint, then serve.

If the refrigerator is full, buy lots of ice, stand the bottles of wine, water or juice in a container such as a large cool-box, then pack ice all around them. Pour in enough water to immerse the bottles. Put the container in the bath or shower cubicle (hide it behind the shower curtain) and leave for 1 hour – the bottles will be perfectly chilled and there is no need to keep opening and shutting the refrigerator door. For a really large party, fill the whole bath with ice and water and immerse all the bottles. Just pull out the plug after everyone leaves.

moroccan mint tea

Mint tea is very soothing after a spicy meal. Don't use spearmint – it will taste like mouthwash.

1½ heaped tablespoons green tea leaves

a handful of whole mint leaves (not spearmint)

about 150–180 g sugar, or to taste

Makes about 1 litre: serves 6

Heat the teapot with just-boiled water. Tip out the water, add the tea leaves and pour a little boiling water over them just to moisten. Swirl around, then quickly pour the water out again, taking care not to lose any leaves. Add a good handful of fresh mint (the sugar is traditionally added at this stage, but leave it out or serve it later). Pour about 1 litre boiling water over the mint and moistened tea leaves. Put on the lid and leave to infuse for 5–8 minutes. Pour into warmed glasses and top with a few extra mint leaves. Hand the sugar around separately.

spiced tea

A deliciously fragrant change from the norm and especially reviving after a long winter's walk, you can make this as strong or as weak as you like. Sometimes I add a teaspoon of condensed milk to each cup – no need for sugar.

1 cinnamon stick

3 cloves

1 star anise

3–4 cardamom pods, lightly crushed

1 heaped tablespoon Indian leaf tea, such as Darjeeling or Assam

To serve (optional)

sugar

milk

Serves 6

Put the cinnamon, cloves, star anise and cardamom pods in a saucepan, add 1 litre water and bring to the boil. Reduce the heat, cover and simmer gently for 5 minutes, then stir in the loose tea. Stir well, cover and leave to infuse for 5 minutes. Strain into a warmed teapot, and serve as it is, or with sugar and milk.

really good coffee

Proper coffee is very easy to make – and you don't need special pots or hissing machines, just a heatproof jug and a fine tea strainer. Hot milk makes all the difference for those who take milk in their coffee; it produces a drink that is almost velvety and keeps hot. Freshly ground coffee is important (freeze the bag after opening, then use straight from frozen). Espresso coffee will take a little longer to settle.

2 tablespoons medium-ground coffee per person

boiling water

hot milk

Pour some hot water into a heatproof jug to warm it up. Empty out and add the appropriate amount of coffee per person. Pour on enough recently boiled water just to cover the coffee grounds. Stir and leave for 1 minute to infuse.

Top up with 300 ml just-boiled water per person and stir well. Cover and let brew for 5 minutes. Either strain through the tea strainer into cups or into another warmed jug. Add hot (not boiled) milk, if using. The coffee will have a *crema* or creamy foam on top if you have followed all the steps correctly, and will have a full, rich flavour.

basics and standbys

a selection of pestos

Liven up soups, use to spread on grilled food or hot toast, stir into a casserole or make a dressing for a salad – pestos are so versatile. Once made and stored in a jar, make sure you level the surface each time you use it, then re-cover with olive oil to keep out the air. Pesto freezes well, so when the best basil is around in summer, I freeze it in ice-cube trays, then keep the cubes in plastic bags. Don't thaw the cubes – just let them melt into whatever's cooking. For basil pesto, see page 64.

walnut and rocket pesto

50 g rocket

1 garlic clove

50 g shelled walnuts

75 g fresh goats' cheese

6 tablespoons olive oil
(or half olive oil, half walnut oil)

freshly ground black pepper

Serves 4

Put all the ingredients in a food processor and blend until smooth, scraping down any bits that cling to the side of the bowl. Spoon into a jar, cover with a thin layer of olive oil to exclude the air, then refrigerate for up to 2 weeks.

basil and lemongrass pesto

1 garlic clove, peeled

1 stalk of lemongrass, chopped

55 g macadamia nuts

55 g fresh basil leaves (no stalks)

1 tablespoon sesame oil

150 ml good olive oil, plus extra to cover

sea salt and freshly ground black pepper

Serves 4

Put the garlic, lemongrass and nuts in a food processor and blend until finely ground. Then add the basil, followed by the sesame and olive oils. Spoon into a jar, cover with a thin layer of olive oil to exclude the air, then refrigerate for up to 2 weeks.

tomato and chilli pesto

1 large red pepper

55 g fresh basil leaves (no stalks)

1 garlic clove, crushed

2 tablespoons pine nuts, toasted

2 very ripe tomatoes

6 sun-dried tomatoes in oil, drained

3 tablespoons tomato purée

1 teaspoon mild chilli powder

55 g freshly grated Parmesan or aged pecorino cheese

150 ml extra virgin olive oil

Serves 6–8

Grill the whole pepper, turning until blackened all over. Peel off most of the blackened skin, pull out the stalk and scrape out the seeds. Put in a food processor with the basil, garlic, pine nuts, tomatoes, sun-dried tomatoes, tomato purée, chilli powder and Parmesan and blend until smooth. With the machine running, slowly pour in the olive oil until well blended. Spoon into a jar, cover with a thin layer of olive oil to exclude the air, and refrigerate for up to 2 weeks.

thai curry pastes and harissa sauce

Thai curry pastes and Tunisian harissa sauce are indispensable. Keep them in either the refrigerator or freezer (freeze in ice-cube trays and press out into thick plastic bags – double-wrap them as they are quite pungent). Homemade pastes knock the spots off the bought variety – and you will be in total control of the heat. You can add small amounts to soups and stews or spread them on fish, meat and chicken for grilling.

red thai curry paste

4 large fresh red chillies, trimmed

3 shallots or 1 medium onion, peeled

6 garlic cloves

2 tablespoons chopped fresh coriander stem and root (no leaves)

1 teaspoon finely grated lime zest

½ stalk of lemongrass, coarsely chopped

1.25 cm piece of fresh ginger, peeled and coarsely chopped

1 teaspoon dried shrimp paste (blachan) or anchovy paste or 3 anchovy fillets

2 teaspoons ground coriander

1 teaspoon ground cumin

1 tablespoon sweet paprika

½ teaspoon freshly ground black pepper

2 tablespoons peanut oil

Makes enough for 6 servings

Cut the chillies in half (wear rubber gloves if you like), remove the seeds and put the flesh in a food processor. Add the remaining ingredients and blend until as smooth as possible, scraping down a couple of times.

green thai curry paste

4 large fresh green chillies, trimmed

3 shallots or 1 medium onion, peeled

6 garlic cloves

3–4 tablespoons chopped fresh coriander leaves

1 tablespoon finely grated lime zest and juice of 1 unwaxed lime

½ stalk of lemongrass, coarsely chopped

1.25 cm piece of fresh ginger, peeled and coarsely chopped

1 teaspoon dried shrimp paste (blachan) or anchovy paste or 3 anchovy fillets

2 teaspoons ground coriander

1 teaspoon ground cumin

½ teaspoon freshly ground black pepper

2 tablespoons peanut oil

Makes enough for 6 servings

Make in the same way as Red Curry Paste.

Note If keeping either paste in the refrigerator, spoon into a jar, making sure there are no air pockets, and cover with a layer of oil. Seal and refrigerate for up to 1 month, or freeze as described above for up to 6 months. Always fry pastes for a few minutes in a little hot oil before using.

harissa sauce

75 g dried mild and hot chillies

1 medium red pepper

1 small garlic clove

1 teaspoon coriander seeds

1 teaspoon caraway seeds

1 teaspoon sea salt

3–4 tablespoons olive oil

Makes about 250 ml

Soak the dried chillies in boiling water for 30 minutes. Roast or grill the red pepper until charred. Rub off the skin and remove the seeds.

Drain the chillies and put in a food processor with the pepper, garlic, coriander and caraway seeds, salt and olive oil. Blend until smooth.

Spoon into a jar, packing down carefully to exclude any air pockets. Pour over a thin layer of olive oil to cover the surface, cover and label.

caramelized onion confit

This confit is the ultimate relish to pile into a grilled steak sandwich and serve with a coarse pâté or a chunk of cheese. I sometimes use blackcurrant jam with a dash or vodka instead of the cassis, and it works very well indeed – sometimes you just have to be creative with what you have.

125 g unsalted butter
750 g red onions, sliced
120 ml sherry or wine vinegar
150 g caster sugar
3 tablespoons crème de cassis (blackcurrant liqueur)
300 ml full-bodied dry red wine
sea salt and freshly ground black pepper

Makes 500 ml

Melt the butter in a frying pan, add the onions and vinegar, cover and simmer for 10 minutes until soft. Add the sugar, increase the heat and cook, stirring, until the onions start to caramelize and the liquid has evaporated. Add the cassis and wine, and cook gently, uncovered, for 20 minutes until all the liquid has evaporated. Add salt and pepper to taste, then spoon into a jar, seal and store in the refrigerator for up to 1 month.

Variation Simple Onion Confit
Melt 50 g unsalted butter in a frying pan and add 2 large sliced onions. Stir to coat with the butter, add 2 tablespoons water, cover and cook over a gentle heat for 10 minutes. Uncover, sprinkle with 2 teaspoons caster sugar and 1 tablespoon balsamic vinegar and increase the heat. Cook over brisk heat for about another 10 minutes, stirring from time to time, but watching it like a hawk. The onions should start to turn a beautiful rich brown colour – if not, just cook a little longer. Set aside when cooked.

black olive tapenade

My recipe for this traditional Provençal spread has a more intense, almost smoky flavour.

1 small sweet red pepper
3 garlic cloves, unpeeled
250 g black olives, preferably wrinkled Greek-style ones, pitted
2–3 tablespoons salted capers or capers in vinegar, rinsed
12 anchovy fillets in oil or 1 small can tuna in oil, drained
about 150 ml olive oil
lemon juice, to taste
freshly ground black pepper

Makes about 600 ml

Cook the red pepper and garlic under a hot grill for about 15 minutes, until completely charred all over (or roast in a hot oven). Let cool, then rub the skin off the pepper (do not wash) and remove the stalk and seeds. Peel the skin off the garlic. Put the pepper, garlic, olives, capers and anchovies in a food processor and work until coarsely chopped. With the machine running, slowly add the olive oil until you have a fairly smooth, dark paste. Add lemon juice and pepper to taste. Transfer to a jar, cover with a layer of olive oil to exclude the air, and keep for up to 1 month.

foolproof focaccia

The secret of a truly light focaccia lies in making a very soft dough and letting it rise until really light and puffy.

25 g fresh yeast, 1 tablespoon active dried yeast or 1 sachet easy-blend yeast
a pinch of sugar
450 ml warm water
700 g strong plain white flour
100 ml extra virgin olive oil
coarse sea salt, for sprinkling

2 shallow springform cake tins, 25 cm diameter, lightly oiled

Makes 2 loaves, each serves 6–8

Cream the fresh yeast and sugar in a bowl, then whisk in the warm water. Leave for 10 minutes until frothy. For other yeasts, use according to the packet instructions. Sift the flour into a large bowl and make a hollow in the centre. Add the yeast mixture and 3 tablespoons olive oil. Mix until the dough comes together. With clean, dry hands, knead the dough on a lightly floured surface for 5 minutes until smooth, elastic and quite soft. If too soft to handle, knead in a little more flour, but not much – it should be very soft.

Divide the dough in half, shape each piece into a ball, then roll out to 25 cm rounds. Put in the oiled tins, cover with a clean damp cloth or oiled clingfilm and let rise in a warm place for 30 minutes or until very light and puffed up.

Uncover and, using your fingertips, make deep dimples all over the surface of the dough down to the base. Drizzle with the remaining oil. Cover again and let rise once more (30 minutes in a warm place), until doubled in size and very light and puffy. Sprinkle generously with salt. Spray with water and bake in a preheated oven at 200°C (400°F) Gas 6 for 20–25 minutes until golden brown. Spray with water twice during cooking if you can. Transfer to a wire rack to cool. Eat the same day or freeze as soon as it is cool.

oatmeal sodabread

There's no yeast in this bread, so the quicker you make it and get it in the oven, the better it will be. After baking, store in a plastic bag or lidded container to keep it moist. Sodabread is always best eaten warm. Try adding cooked chopped bacon and sage, sun-dried tomatoes and olives, poppyseeds – the list is endless. Bake in a tin or straight on a baking sheet. It freezes very well for up to a month.

about 200 ml milk plus extra for glazing
2 tablespoons lemon juice
225 g wholemeal or granary flour
125 g plain white flour
50 g medium oatmeal
1½ teaspoons bicarbonate of soda
1½ teaspoons cream of tartar
¾ teaspoon sea salt
40 g unsalted butter

a deep cake tin, 18 cm diameter, lightly brushed with oil

Makes 1 round loaf, 18 cm diameter

Mix the milk with the lemon juice and leave for 5 minutes. Put the flours, oatmeal, bicarbonate of soda, cream of tartar and salt in a large bowl. Mix well, then rub in the butter. Stir the milk into the dry ingredients to form a soft, slightly sticky dough, adding a little extra milk if necessary. Knead very lightly and quickly (this is the secret to a light, crumbly sodabread) until just smooth. Pat out the dough lightly and use to fill the prepared tin. Brush the top with a little milk. Bake in a preheated oven at 220°C (425°F) Gas 7 for about 30 minutes or until the base sounds hollow when given a sharp tap. Do not overcook or the bread will become very dry.

prunes or cherries in armagnac or brandy

Make a huge jar of these to store in the refrigerator. They can be served as they are after a meal or with a scoop of cream or ice cream. They are also good baked into a custard tart or cheesecake and are utterly fab chopped up and stirred into softened chocolate ice cream, then frozen for later.

375 g large sweet pitted prunes or pitted fresh cherries

150 ml Armagnac or brandy

200 ml sweet white wine

1 vanilla pod, split

100 g sugar

a strip of unwaxed lemon zest

1 cinnamon stick

Serves 4

Soak the prunes or cherries overnight in the Armagnac and wine. Lift out the fruit with a slotted spoon and drop into a preserving jar. Pour the wine into a saucepan and add the vanilla pod, sugar, lemon zest and cinnamon. Bring to the boil, then pour over the prunes. Seal immediately, cool and store in the refrigerator for up to 3 months.

a pot of jam

I recently discovered this wonderful way of making small quantities of jam in the microwave.

500 g fresh ripe strawberries, hulled and quartered

350 g sugar with added pectin (sometimes known as 'jam sugar' – see right)

Makes 1½ pots, 500 g each

Put the strawberries in a large bowl with a splash of water. Cover and microwave on FULL for 2 minutes. Carefully uncover and stir in the sugar. Re-cover and cook on FULL for another 2 minutes.

Uncover and stir well to dissolve the sugar. Replace in the microwave uncovered and cook on FULL for 8 minutes.

Test by dropping a teaspoon onto a chilled saucer and chilling in the refrigerator for 10 minutes. If it has set up, pour the jam into clean dry jars and cover. If not, microwave for 4 more minutes, then try the test again. Pour into warm, sterilized jars and seal. After opening, the jam will keep in the refrigerator for up to 2 weeks.

lemon curd

6 large eggs

3 large unwaxed lemons

250 g unsalted butter

500 g caster sugar

Makes about 1 litre

Separate 2 of the eggs (freeze the whites for use at a later date in meringues). Beat the 2 egg yolks with the remaining 4 whole eggs until completely blended.

Finely grate the zest from all the lemons, but squeeze the juice from only 2.

Melt the butter in a bowl set over a saucepan of simmering water, then stir in the sugar. When warm, pour the beaten eggs through a strainer into the saucepan, then add the lemon juice and zest. Cook, stirring all the time for about 20 minutes or until the curd has thickened considerably. If you are brave enough, you can cook this over direct heat, watching that it doesn't get too hot and curdle. Strain into warm, dry, sterilized jars and seal.

Store in the refrigerator for no longer than 3 months absolute maximum.

uncooked freezer raspberry jam

There is no boiling needed for this recipe, so you keep the taste of fresh raspberries. Commercially produced 'jam sugar' is perfect for this – it has added pectin that helps the jam thicken to a soft set. Use 120 ml liquid pectin, if you can't find this special jam sugar.

750 g fresh raspberries

1 kg sugar with added pectin (sometimes known as 'jam sugar')

2 tablespoons freshly squeezed lemon juice

Makes 2 pots, 500 g each

Tip the raspberries into a bowl and crush a bit with a potato masher. Stir in the jam sugar and lemon juice. Cover with clingfilm and heat on MEDIUM in the microwave for about 5 minutes or until warmed through.

Uncover and stir gently to dissolve the sugar, then leave to stand overnight. Alternatively, heat in a saucepan until the sugar has dissolved.

The next day, pot up into freezer containers and freeze – keep one pot in the refrigerator for breakfast tomorrow. After removing from the freezer, store the jam in the refrigerator. Thaw before using.

To sterilize jam jars, wash them in hot, soapy water and rinse in boiling water. Place in a large saucepan and cover with hot water. With the lid on, bring the water to the boil and continue boiling for 15 minutes. Turn off the heat, then leave the jars in the hot water until just before they are to be filled. Invert the jars onto a clean cloth to dry. Sterilize the lids for 5 minutes, by boiling, or according to the manufacturer's instructions. The jars should be filled and sealed while still hot.

menu planner

Vegetarian Lunch
- Mushroom, Walnut and Goats' Cheese Tart OR
- Ricotta, Basil and Cherry Tomato Cannelloni
- Caesar Salad
- Really Good Coffee
- Chocolate Chilli Truffles

Summer
- Jellied Bloody Marys with Tapenade Toasts
- Whole Poached Salmon with Sweet and Sour Pickled Cucumber
- Green Rice (hot or cold)
- Hazelnut and Raspberry Pavlova with Hot Chocolate Sauce

Summer in the Garden
- White Sangria
- Jewelled Gazpacho
- Salmon Steaks with Hot Pesto and Tomatoes
- Brown Sugar Meringues OR
- Coffee Panna Cotta

Barbecue Party
- Guacamole and Tortilla Chips
- Moroccan Butterflied Lamb
- Roasted Mediterranean Vegetables
- Barbecued Whole Sweetcorn with Chilli Lime Butter
- Bananas with Sultana Rum Ice Cream

Italian Flavours
- Grilled Goats' Cheese and Rosemary Bruschetta with Baked Garlic Cloves OR
- Tagliolini with Lemon and Green Olives
- Tuscan Chicken
- Perfect Parmesan Mash
- Roasted Mediterranean Vegetables
- Coffee Panna Cotta

Picnic
- Fiery Red Pepper Soup (in a thermos) if it's a cold day
- Real Old-fashioned Lemonade
- Pissaladière
- Tuscan Chicken (cold)
- Mushroom, Walnut and Goats' Cheese Tart
- Fillet of Beef Salad with Thai Dressing
- Cold Noodles with Peanut Sauce
- Lemon Curd Tartlets (fill on site)

Cold Buffet
- Jellied Bloody Marys with Tapenade Toasts
- Baba Ghanoush
- Whole Poached Salmon with Sweet and Sour Pickled Cucumber
- Fillet of Beef Salad with Thai Dressing
- Cold Noodles with Peanut Sauce
- Green Rice (hot or cold)
- Hazelnut and Raspberry Pavlova with Hot Chocolate Sauce
- Fruit Frangipane Tart
- Mango Mousse with Tropical Fruit Salad

Hot Buffet
- A Big Pot of Cassoulet
- Ricotta, Basil and Cherry Tomato Cannelloni
- Tomato and Aubergine Gratin
- Caesar Salad
- Hazelnut and Raspberry Pavlova with Hot Chocolate Sauce

A Crowd of Teenagers
- Oven-roasted Spiced Nuts
- Guacamole and Tortilla Chips
- Baba Ghanoush
- Mexican Pork and Beans
- Prawn Green Curry with Noodles (or with tofu for non-meat eaters)
- Green Rice
- Mango Mousse with Tropical Fruit Salad OR
- Hazelnut and Raspberry Pavlova with Hot Chocolate Sauce

OR
- Tapenade Toasts
- Moules Marinières Feast
- Mango Mousse with Tropical Fruit Salad

Kids Are Coming
- Leek and Potato Soup (with Watercress Purée for adults)
- Perfect Roast Fillet of Beef with Herbed Yorkshire Puddings
- Perfect Mashed Potatoes
- Vichy Carrots
- Petits Pois à la Française

or
- A Big Pot of Cassoulet
- Coffee Panna Cotta OR
- Lemon Curd Tartlets

Taste of the Middle East
- Dukka
- Felafel
- Baba Ghanoush

OR
- Chickpea Chermoula Soup
- Moroccan Butterflied Lamb
- Sesame and Mint Couscous with Winter Vegetables
- Fruit Frangipane Tart
- Moroccan Mint Tea

Asian Angles
- Smoked Salmon and Cucumber Sushi Rolls
- Prawn Green Curry with Noodles (or with tofu for non-meat eaters)
- Fillet of Beef Salad with Thai Dressing
- Cold Noodles with Peanut Sauce
- Mango Mousse with Tropical Fruit Salad
- Chinese Fortune Cookies

Winter Feast
- Chicken Liver Parfait with Bitter Orange and Onion Chutney
- Perfect Roast Beef with Herbed Yorkshire Puddings
- Perfect Mashed Potatoes
- Vichy Carrots
- Petits Pois à la Française
- Mixed Nut Treacle Tart OR
- Chocolate Chilli Truffles

Cosy Comforting Supper
- Leek and Potato Soup with Watercress Purée
- Pot Roast Leg of Lamb with Garlic Sauce OR
- Steak and Wild Mushroom Pies
- Dauphinoise Potatoes
- Tomato and Aubergine Gratin with Tomato and Chilli Pesto
- Bananas with Sultana Rum Ice Cream

Late-Night Supper
- Parmesan and Rosemary Palmiers
- Moules Marinières (have it all ready to cook at the last minute)

OR
- Ricotta, Basil and Cherry Tomato Cannelloni
- Coffee Panna Cotta
- Chocolate Chilli Truffles

index